WHAT IT MEANS TO BE AN AMERICAN

Michael Walzer

Marsilio
New York

This volume copyright © 1992
Marsilio Publishers Corp.
853 Broadway
New York, New York 10003

Distributed in the U.S.A. by
Rizzoli International Publications, Inc.
300 Park Avenue South
New York, New York 10010

ISBN 0-941419-66-5

PRINTED IN THE UNITED STATES OF AMERICA
First Edition

for Dita Shklar
1928-1992

Table of Contents

WHAT IT MEANS
TO BE AN AMERICAN

INTRODUCTION

I

The four essays collected in this small volume deal with the politics of difference in the United States. When I wrote them I was primarily interested in ethnic and religious difference. What may well turn out to be the harder questions of class, gender, and race figure only marginally in these essays. (I have written about them elsewhere, but in a different vein, without referring to the idea of difference.) Cultural diversity and religious toleration are American success stories, relative, at least, to the continuing and shameful inequalities connected to and in important ways attributable to capitalism, sexism, and racism. Insofar as the United States is a society of *voluntary* immigrants – excluding, then, the Indians, who were conquered and the blacks, who were coercively transported – it is one of the world's better societies: open, pluralist, and (relatively, again) egalitarian. The essays that follow describe the conditions of this achievement and something of its specific character.

In this introduction, my aim is rather more general: I want to give a comparative and theoretical account of the politics of difference and suggest how it might work in social settings where immigration and cultural pluralism are already and where they aren't yet of major importance. What can be called "the new tribalism" in Central and Eastern Europe (though it is also very old and not without parallels in the West) provides the immediate occasion of my comparison: "tribalism" contrasted with "multiculturalism." I will also try to say something about the ways in which the European Community might or might not be a "United States of Europe" and about the ways in which the United States can and cannot be a national community.

II

Examined across time, the politics of difference has three moments, which I propose to call the moments of articulation, negotiation, and incorporation. The sequence is by no means inevitable. One can imagine the first moment without the second and third or with a different second and third: for example, articulation, war, and permanent division. And it may well be true in the United States that "incorporation" both begins and ends the sequence – the naturalization of the immigrants preceding the discovery of their collective "roots" and the creation of a pluralism of groups and cultures. But the three moments have a certain normative logic. If they aren't a literal summary of our experience, they are at least an expression of our hopes.

1) Articulation. The politics of difference begins when a group of people, previously invisible, repressed, and fearful, insists on its value as a group and on the solidarity of its members, and demands some form of public recognition. Usually, the members (or the militants among them) speak out in

response to an effort, launched from the outside though often with internal support, to absorb them into some larger entity. Czarist Russification or the American "melting pot" are obvious examples of efforts of this sort, but it makes sense to include among them the more universalist programs of leftist parties aiming at the transcendence of all parochial identities. For what is articulated in this first moment is precisely the devalued parochialism of a given group. And the point of the articulation is to reject universalist transcendence as much as particularist domination. It's not only that Latvians (for example) don't want to be Russians or Soviet citizens; they also don't want—not yet, at least—to be turned into global citizens. They want to affirm their Latvian identity and claim the political right to protect and foster that identity. In much the same way, black Americans don't want to be Americans simply, nor men and women without qualification; they want to give the adjective "black" real linguistic and cultural force. (Similarly again, feminist movements don't aim to recreate women in a male image; nor do their activists want—not yet, at least—to participate in a genderless humanity. They want to affirm the value of their own experience and sensibility.)

Articulation has a literal meaning: it gives voice to difference. And once difference has been expressed in this affirmative and self-affirming way, it can no longer be denied, abolished, assimilated, or transcended. It is simply *there,* a feature of the social world, and from now on any refusal to recognize it will itself be recognized as an act of oppression. But what will be the sound of all these new voices? Cacophony seems more likely than harmony. And, indeed, multi-ethnicity and multiculturalism are, in their beginnings, cacophonous – harsh and jangling, exactly like the dissidence of Protestant dissent in the sixteenth and seventeenth centuries. There are a large number of repressed groups, or groups that claim to have been repressed, and the further claims they make are often radically contradictory and difficult to sort out. The process of sorting them out is the second moment of the politics of difference.

2) Negotiation. It is always a surprise when repressed groups fail to recognize the general category from which they have just escaped. Again and again, they act as if they are the only or the last victims of repression, and they claim rights and entitlements that restrict the rights and entitlements of the groups that come next, their neighbors in repression or the minorities in their own midst. I suppose that this is the kind of behavior that is called human, all-too-human. Because of it, the articulation of difference, however liberating, is also very dangerous. So there begins a long and painful negotiation, through which each group must come to acknowledge that its limits are set by the legitimacy of the others. The limits themselves take many different forms. In international society, they are most often borders, where passports can be checked and customs collected. In domestic society, they are restraints on the use of public resources (like the American "wall" between church and state) or on the representation of group beliefs in the ceremonies of the civic culture or the policies of the state.

The purpose of the limits is to make peaceful co-existence possible in a society of nations or in a pluralist civil society – a "social union of social unions," in the phrase of the American philosopher John Rawls. But there is also the hope, not always vivid in the minds of the negotiators, that the process of negotiation will give rise to a shared commitment to tolerance, equality, and mutual aid. The fact that the process is ongoing and probably endless testifies to the character of international and civil society: these are realms of fragmentation. And the more successful the articulation of difference is, the more fragmented they are. But the fragments are neither morally nor materially self-sufficient. So the negotiations that fix their boundaries also explore possibilities for boundary crossings. They draw lines, so to speak, on the social map, and then seek to turn these into dotted lines, incorporating difference in some larger whole.

3) Incorporation. Old and unjust incorporations precede the politics of difference and make it necessary. Empires incorporate captive nations; religious or cultural establishments dominate and seek to assimilate minority groups. Articulation shatters these ancient patterns, and negotiation replaces them with their liberated, dissociated pieces. But the replacement won't work for long unless the different pieces are somehow brought together. They are in need of economic assistance and political cooperation. Hence the negotiating process, if it goes well, will tend over time to expand its horizons, reaching toward free trade zones, economic unions, political blocs and federations in international society and toward religious and cultural pluralism, regional autonomy, group representation, affirmative action, and new forms of citizenship in domestic society. These are, ideally at least, non-repressive modes of incorporation – different modes for different cases. It would be odd if the politics of difference had some singular and uniform outcome.

In fact, we can't identify or describe any such outcome, even in ideal terms. What was asserted in the first moment remains true in the third: there is no transcendence of cultural, religious, and national particularity. There is no "higher" social formation than the local group, no historically necessary universalism beyond the newly articulated universe of difference. There are larger, more inclusive social formations and identities – themselves of different kinds – and these are certainly worth working for and defending. But we have to defend them without metaphysical or metahistorical reference. We are reduced to our best arguments: secular, pragmatic, inconclusive. Our differences will be expressed even in the schemes we devise for incorporating difference.

I want to stress that the work of incorporation can only begin after we have made our peace with the newly liberated groups. This doesn't have to be an uncritical peace; nor need the terms be the same for the different groups. We can make judgements about their character and conduct. But there is today no democratic way of opposing the politics of difference. Fragmentation is, for now at least, the vehicle of democracy. We can see this most clearly in the East, where active resistance to tyranny and also the more passive and widespread recalcitrance and evasion that undermined the Stalinist regimes from within were fueled in large part by particularist passions. These passions will have to be restrained if the politics of difference is to have a democratic outcome. But they can't legitimately be restrained unless they are also, partially, satisfied.

III

The crucial problem of the politics of difference is to encompass the actually existing differences within some overarching political structure. This structure takes a variety of forms, which depend on the historical sources and social character of the differences in question. I will describe two of the more likely forms, one of them the subject of this book, the other sketched here, briefly, for purposes of comparison.

The first fits the case of the United States, though it is repeated, with many variations, in all the immigrant societies of the Americas and the Pacific (Canada, Brazil, New Zealand, etc.). What is critical here is the territorial dispersion of the immigrant "tribes" – national and ethnic groups, races, religious communities. With the exception of black slaves, immigrants to the United States came one by one, or family by family, and though they sought out (and were sometimes locked into) segregated neighborhoods, they avoided any larger segregation, moving freely around the country and creating radically mixed cities and states. Hence no one group was able to determine for long the character even of local governments. In some general way, the political culture of the country as a whole was English and Protestant, but this culture was never firmly established either in the symbols or the substance of law and policy. Nor did the immigrant groups assimilate entirely into the dominant culture. To varying degrees, they resisted it, sustaining separate cultural identities, so that the United States took shape as a "nation of nationalities" (the phrase comes from a defense of pluralism by the American Jewish political theorist Horace Kallen, writing in the 1910s).

At the same time, most of the immigrants became citizens and in this very important sense "Americans." The United States is a political nation of cultural nationalities. Citizenship is separated from every sort of particularism: the state is nationally, ethnically, racially, and religiously neutral. At least, this is true in principle, and whenever neutrality is violated, there is likely to be a principled fight against the violation. The expression of difference is confined to civil society, where the various "nationalities" have produced an extraor-dinary array of organizations for religious worship, welfare provision, education, culture, and mutual protection. These organizations are run on a voluntary basis; most of them are precariously established, skimpily funded, always at risk. A great deal of energy is invested here – energy that in other societies is drawn into political life. The result is an open, lively, and highly contentious civil society and a not very robust citizenship.

It is a hard question – much debated in America today – what the right social-political balance is in a pluralist society. I argue in several of the essays that follow for a much stronger American citizenship, for a political community of engaged and active men and women. This is an argument that might well be joined today by many of the critics of American mul-ticulturalism. The articulation of difference, they might say, has gone very far in the United States and the negotiation of difference has become increasingly problematic. The result-ing politics is too close to a zero-sum game, in which the claims of one group can only be vindicated at the expense of one or more of the others. There is too little sense of a com-mon good. And yet all the groups, precisely because of their dispersion and inter-mixing, share a common political space, whose safety, healthfulness, beauty, and accessibility are col-lective values. Only citizens can defend these values – and only citizens who participate in a larger politics will be fully capable of such a defense, that is, both committed to it and competent enough to make it a success. The stronger the par-ticularist identities of individual men and women are, the stronger their citizenship must be. For then, though individ-uals will be divided ("hyphenated"), the nation of nationali-ties, the social union of social unions, will be held together.

10

I am inclined to think this a good argument and a useful response to those advocates of multiculturalism who are really local nationalists, less interested in the negotiation of difference that in the aggrandizement of their particular group. But my own argument in these essays takes a somewhat different direction, for it seems to me that our singular citizenship and our pluralized culture have, in fact, a common enemy. Both are threatened by a radicalized ideology of individualism and an anti-politics of privatization. "Do your own thing" is an ethic that drives hard against the necessary collectivism of both politics and culture. Citizens are not effective one by one but only when they are bound together in states or freely associated in parties, interest groups, and social movements. And culture is not sustained by private men and women but by families, nations, and communities of faith. These are different sorts of associations, but they co-exist in civil society and they are by no means rivalrous. They are likely to flourish together, stimulated by each other's success, feeding on each other's members. There is considerable evidence, for example (think of the history of English Methodism or of black Baptism in America), that people active in their churches are readily recruited for political action. By contrast, individuals who are privately absorbed are likely to be inactive both in their particularist communities and in the larger community.

Engaged men and women tend to be multiply engaged. This is especially true in American society where citizenship is not supported by a singular ethnic or religious identity but is instead mediated by a diversity of identities, each with its own organizations. No doubt, this mediation is often tense and difficult: the more groups, the more militants, the more arguments, the more tumult. And then publicists and prophets warn us that the country is falling apart. But the real alternative to tumult, under American conditions, is not unity but passivity – the disengagement of private individuals from one another and hence from any meaningful politics. Of course, it is easier to govern a culture of privacy than a culture of engagement. And the difficulties created by the second of these only increase as more and more groups articulate their interests or values and join in the process of negotiating their differences. The argument of these essays, however, is that this process lies at the heart of democratic politics in a society like ours. Our union is and will probably always be tumultuous, for we hold together our "nation of nationalities" by enlisting the energy of the different nationalities in the work of the singular nation.

IV

Exactly what this work involves, what Americans can and cannot do to hold themselves together, is best understood if we consider briefly the experience of contemporary nation-states. Political incorporation takes a very different form in (and among) societies older than our own, whose members are not immigrants or, at least, not recent immigrants, but constitute, instead, ancient, long-standing, territorially based communities. Of course, communities of this sort have their own internal (social and ideological) differences; nor are ethnic, racial, or religious minorities ever absent from the countries they rule. But where there is an anciently established majority, politics is bound to draw on its history and culture and then to take on something of its particularity – as in a nation-state like Poland, say, or a religious republic like Iran.

Now the state won't be neutral in the American style: the official calendar, the rituals and ceremonies of public life, the education provided in the public schools will all be influenced by a particular national or religious tradition. And they will in turn reinforce that same tradition, providing it with a kind of political support that no American notion or religion gets (or should get).

There is nothing necessarily unjust about these connections between nationality or faith on the one hand and political institutions and practices on the other, so long as ethnic and religious minorities are protected and the rights of citizenship are fully available to their members. It is not necessary, despite Rousseau's argument in his *Constitution of Poland,* to be a Pole *and nothing else* in order to be a loyal Polish citizen. And this is true even if the meaning of citizenship is partially determined by the historical experience of the Poles and partially expressed in symbols drawn from that experience.

But the inclusion of strangers is obviously harder in countries ruled by ancient majorities than it is in countries founded and ruled by immigrants. Perhaps countries of the first sort can imitate countries of the second by making room for strangers in civil society (this is easiest when the economy is expanding and times are good). Politics, however, is of greater weight in everyday life if it is nationally or religiously connected – and powered, as it were, by its connections. A greater proportion of the work that needs doing in the areas of welfare, education, and culture will be done in and through the nation-state. The state bureaucracy will play a larger role, and secondary associations are most likely to flourish if they are (like political parties and movements) aimed at the state. Communal groups whose purposes are religious, cultural, or philanthropic will attract less interest and fewer active members than they do in the United States. "Private" schools, which add to the general curriculum some specific sectarian content, will attract fewer students.

The relation of individuals to the state will be more direct in national than in multi-national settings; group mediations will be reduced in importance. And so privatization will be less of a threat to citizenship and culture. Individual citizens will, of course, participate more or less actively in public life, but even the least active will feel themselves politically attached. The attachment will seem almost natural: unproblematic and easy (it is hard to imagine the French or Italian equivalent of an Americanization campaign). One might want to alter the balance here in favor of civil society and its associations—in order to facilitate the inclusion of strangers or the local activism of ordinary citizens. But the existence of a majority nation will always make for a strong central state, and so it will always be necessary to insist upon the accessibility of the state to men and women of different nations—minorities, refugees, guest workers—who live within its borders. They may choose to involve themselves more in their own ethnic or religious associations than in politics, but that should be, as much as it can be, a real choice. This argument applies, however, only to residents, and so it points to a further question: who should be admitted to residence, who should live *here, among us?*

Immigration is a genuine problem in countries with ancient majorities—as it is not, or ought not to be, in immigrant societies like ours. For the members of the majority nation or religion won't want to be overwhelmed in their own country. They will favor immigrants who resemble themselves and seem likely to blend into the established culture. The arguments about immigration in contemporary Europe regularly exhibit a xenophobic or racist character. But this isn't the necessary character of every argument in favor of restrictions on the admission of foreigners. We can test the men and women who defend restrictions by asking them how they mean to treat those foreigners already admitted and how they want to deal with the countries from which the immigrants come: are they ready for political cooperation and serious economic assistance? Americans expand their solidarity by taking new nations into their state (Slavs, Italians, and Jews in the late nineteenth and early twentieth centuries, Hispanics and Asians today). Europeans are more likely to expand their solidarity by forming economic unions or political federations with other nation-states. In the first case, the politics of difference produces new, hyphenated identities (Asian-American) in place of the old singularities. In the second, it produces a new singular identity (European, say) alongside and in addition to the old one.

The United States is not most importantly a union of states but of nations, races, and religions, all of them dispersed and inter-mixed, without ground of their own. The European Community is (or is on its way to becoming) a more literal "United States," for it is precisely a union of states – or of nations on their own ground. Immigration among these states, like the existence of national or religious minorities within them, produces something more like an American society. But the fundamental contrast between Europe and America is likely to remain: we might think of it as a contrast between territorially grounded ("tribal") and groundless ("multicultural") difference. The two require dissimilar negotiations, which give rise in turn to dissimilar unions. Nonetheless, they reflect a common moral and political imperative.

In neither of these cases is there any world-historical cancellation or supersession of parochial identities. The two represent different ways (not better or worse ways) of accommodating difference. The moral principle common to both is that difference ought to be accommodated. The precise form of the accommodation has to be worked out politically, as the actual differences are articulated, negotiated, and incorporated. In the European case, especially in the East, old unities (like Yugoslavia and the Soviet Union) must be disrupted before new incorporations are possible. And the disruptions have been painful, often bloody. The necessary new boundaries are hard to find or agree on, the rights of minorities hard to establish. But the resulting states are going to be nation-states, not multi-national states, and they will come together, if they do, like Italy and Germany in the European Union, not like Italian-Americans and German-Americans in the USA.

Watching this long process, with all its attendant brutalities, we may, perhaps, feel nostalgic for the imperial (or even the totalitarian) politics that preceded the articulation of difference. What is gained by articulation, someone might ask, if the subsequent negotiations continually break down, turning into a kind of armed diplomacy and irregular warfare? But the repression of difference had its own characteristic brutalities, and it was necessarily, inherently, anti-democratic. Articulation can be the beginning of democracy – if only the new states are able to imagine and move toward a common life or, better, a number of common lives, that embrace difference and give it room to flourish.

V

How are we, in the United States, to embrace difference and maintain a common life? Readers of this introduction and of the essays that follow will quickly realize that I am less nervous about this question than many contemporary writers and critics. There are more important and harder questions that Americans have to answer, having to do with economic decline, growing inequality, the condition of the underclass. Against that background, the debate over multiculturalism is almost a diversion. Still, we are in the midst of a second "great immigration," comparable to that of the years 1890-1910, multiplying American cultures and opening the way for new articulations of difference. So this is a good time to reassert the twinned American values of a singular citizenship and a radically pluralist civil society. That reassertion is my purpose in these essays. Anticipating and drawing on their arguments (though they are not policy oriented essays), I will try here to provide a brief checklist of the principles and projects that are most obviously necessary to it.

1) Don't shut the gates. This is not Europe; we are a society of immigrants, and the experience of leaving a homeland and coming to this new place is an almost universal "American" experience. It should be celebrated. But the celebration will be inauthentic and hypocritical if we are busy building walls around our country. Whatever regulation is necessary – we can argue about that – the flow of people, the material base of multiculturalism, should not be cut off.

2) Strengthen the public schools, and focus them – as much as this can be done in so decentralized a system – on two

things: first, the history and contemporary forms of democratic politics, and second, the immigrant experience. The first of these is bound to be, in the current jargon, "Eurocentric," for democracy is in fact largely a European creation. The second should be multicultural, but honestly so: the story that needs telling is not only about how the different ethnic and religious cultures are in fact *different* but also about how they have been commonly transformed by their new American home – Americanized without being melted down or assimilated.

3) Recognize the extent to which American citizens acquire political competence within secondary and often parochial associations. Civil society is for us the ground of democratic politics, and this is ground that must be tended by the state. Regulation and subsidy are both necessary, but so is active cooperation of a sort that might be inappropriate in a less divided society. Thus, we ought to have (in my view) a universal health care system, but much of the care should be delivered, as it is today, in hospitals or nursing homes sponsored and run by one or another religious community. The specific mix of general and particular will have to be worked out politically.

4) However it is worked out, maintain the neutrality of the state by making sure that all eligible particularisms are represented in the mix and that the generality is truly general, itself without any specific ethnic, racial, or religious character. The United States cannot be a Christian republic in the way that Iran is an Islamic republic. But the institutions that various Christian groups have built in civil society, providing cultural, educational, and health services, can be (indirectly) assisted by the state, with tax exemptions, matching grants, and so on – so long as other groups receive a similar assistance.

5) Create a more participatory politics, because it is the exercise of political rights that gives them value in the eyes of

the citizens. It enhances the citizen's commitment to the larger community. "Give him something to do for the public," wrote John Stuart Mill, ". . .and his ideas and feelings are taken out of [their] narrow circle. . . He is made to feel that, besides the interests which separate him from his fellow-citizens, he has interests which connect him with them; that not only is the common weal his weal, but that it partly depends upon his exertions."

6) Don't give way to the silliness and intermittent nastiness that inevitably accompanies democratic politics in multicultural societies. Autocratic and aristocratic politics have their own characteristic forms of silliness and nastiness, but the democratic forms are noisier, and sometimes we are inclined to appeasement, if only for the sake of a little quiet. But the right response to demagogues and cults, to bizarre doctrines of racial superiority and unlikely tales of conspiracy, is ostracism, avoidance, rejection. Skinheads and Sun people will always be with us, but in a society as rich and troubled as ours, we must deal with them and move on; we have bigger problems than they pose and more interesting things to talk about.

WHAT DOES IT MEAN
TO BE AN "AMERICAN"?

There is no country called America. We live in the United States *of America,* and we have appropriated the adjective "American" even though we can claim no exclusive title to it. Canadians and Mexicans are also Americans, but they have adjectives more obviously their own, and we have none. Words like "unitarian" and "unionist" won't do; our sense of ourselves is not captured by the mere fact of our union, however important that is. Nor will "statist," even "united statist," serve our purposes; a good many of the citizens of the United States are antistatist. Other countries, wrote the "American" political theorist Horace Kallen, get their names from the people, or from one of the peoples, who inhabit them. "The United States, on the other hand, has a peculiar anonymity."[1] It is a name that doesn't even pretend to tell us who lives here. Anybody can live here, and just about everybody does—men and women from all the world's peoples. (The *Harvard Encyclopedia of American Ethnic Groups* begins with Acadians and Afghans and ends with Zoroastrians.[2]) It is peculiarly easy to

1 Horace M. Kallen, *Culture and Democracy in the United States* (New York: Boni & Liveright, 1924), p. 51.

2 *Harvard Encyclopedia of American Ethnic Groups,* ed. Stephan Thernstrom (Cambridge, Mass.: Harvard University Press, 1980).

become an American. The adjective provides no reliable information about the origins, histories, connections, or cultures of those whom it designates. What does it say, then, about their political allegiance?

Patriotism and Pluralism

American politicians engage periodically in a fierce competition to demonstrate their patriotism. This is an odd competition, surely, for in most countries the patriotism of politicians is not an issue. There are other issues, and this question of political identification and commitment rarely comes up; loyalty to the *patrie,* the fatherland (or motherland), is simply assumed. Perhaps it isn't assumed here because the United States isn't a *patrie.* Americans have never spoken of their country as a fatherland (or a motherland). The kind of natural or organic loyalty that we (rightly or wrongly) recognize in families doesn't seem to be a feature of our politics. When American politicians invoke the metaphor of family they are usually making an argument about our mutual responsibilities and welfarist obligations, and among Americans, that is a controversial argument.[3] One can be an American patriot without believing in the mutual responsibilities of American citizens – indeed, for some Americans disbelief is a measure of one's patriotism.

Similarly, the United States isn't a "homeland" (where a national family might dwell), not, at least, as other countries are, in casual conversation and unreflective feeling. It is a country of immigrants who, however grateful they are for

3 Mario Cuomo's speech at the 1984 Democratic party convention provides a nice example of this sort of argument.

this new place, still remember the old places. And their children know, if only intermittently, that they have roots elsewhere. They, no doubt, are native grown, but some awkward sense of newness here, or of distant oldness, keeps the tongue from calling this land "home." The older political uses of the word "home," common in Great Britain, have never taken root here: home counties, home station, Home Office, home rule. To be "at home" in America is a personal matter: Americans have homesteads and homefolks and hometowns, and each of these is an endlessly interesting topic of conversation. But they don't have much to say about a common or communal home.

Nor is there a common *patrie*, but rather many different ones — a multitude of fatherlands (and motherlands). For the children, even the grandchildren, of the immigrant generation, one's *patrie*, the "native land of one's ancestors," is somewhere else. The term "Native Americans" designates the very first immigrants, who got here centuries before any of the others. At what point do the rest of us, native grown, become natives? The question has not been decided; for the moment, however, the language of nativism is mostly missing (it has never been dominant in American public life), even when the political reality is plain to see. Alternatively, nativist language can be used against the politics of nativism, as in these lines of Horace Kallen, the theorist of an anonymous America:

> Behind [the individual] in time and tremendously in him in quality are his ancestors; around him in space are his relatives and kin, carrying in common with him the inherited organic set from a remoter common ancestry. In all these he lives and moves and has his being. They constitute his, literally, *natio,* the inwardness of his nativity.[4]

4 Kallen, *Culture and Democracy,* p. 94.

But since there are so many "organic sets" (language is deceptive here: Kallen's antinativist nativism is cultural, not biological), none of them can rightly be called "American." Americans have no inwardness of their own; they look inward only by looking backward.

According to Kallen, the United States is less importantly a union of states than it is a union of ethnic, racial, and religious groups—a union of otherwise unrelated "natives." What is the nature of this union? The Great Seal of the United States carries the motto *E pluribus unum*, "From many, one," which seems to suggest that manyness must be left behind for the sake of oneness. Once there were many, now the many have merged or, in Israel Zangwell's classic image, been melted down into one. But the Great Seal presents a different image: the "American" eagle holds a sheaf of arrows. Here there is no merger or fusion but only a fastening, a putting together: many-in-one. Perhaps the adjective "American" describes this kind of oneness. We might say, tentatively, that it points to the citizenship, not the nativity or nationality, of the men and women it designates. It is a political adjective, and its politics is liberal in the strict sense: generous, tolerant, ample, accommodating—it allows for the survival, even the enhancement and flourishing, of manyness.

On this view, appropriately called "pluralist," the word "from" on the Great Seal is a false preposition. There is no movement from many to one, but rather a simultaneity, a coexistence—once again, many-in-one. But I don't mean to suggest a mystery here, as in the Christian conception of a God who is three-in-one. The language of pluralism is sometimes a bit mysterious—thus Kallen's description of America as a "nation of nationalities" or John Rawls's account of the liberal state as a "social union of social unions"—but it lends itself to a rational unpacking.[5] A sheaf of arrows is not, after all, a mysterious entity. We can find analogues in the earliest forms of social organization: tribes composed of many clans, clans composed of many families. The conflicts of loyalty and obligation, inevitable products of pluralism, must arise in these cases too. And yet, they are not exact analogues of the American case, for tribes and clans lack Kallen's "anonymity." American pluralism is, as we shall see, a peculiarly modern phenomenon – not mysterious but highly complex.

In fact, the United States is not a literal "nation of nationalities" or a "social union of social unions." At least, the singular nation or union is not constituted by, it is not a combination or fastening together of, the plural nationalities or unions. In some sense, it includes them; it provides a framework for their coexistence; but they are not its parts. Nor are the individual states, in any significant sense, the parts that make up the United States. The parts are individual men and women. The United States is an association of citizens. Its "anonymity" consists in the fact that these citizens don't transfer their collective name to the association. It never happened that a group of people called Americans came together to form a political society called America. The people are Americans only by virtue of having come together. And whatever identity they had before becoming Americans, they retain (or, better, they are free to retain) afterward. There is, to be sure, another view of Americanization, which holds that the process requires for its success the mental erasure of all previous identities – forgetfulness or even, as one enthusiast wrote in 1918, "absolute forgetfulness."[6] But on the pluralist

5 *Ibid*, p. 122 (cf. 116); John Rawls, *A Theory of Justice* (Cambridge, Mass.: Harvard University Press, 1971), p. 527.

6 Quoted in Kallen, *Culture and Democracy*, p. 138; the writer was superintendent of New York's public schools.

view, Americans are allowed to remember who they were and to insist, also, on *what else they are.*

They are not, however, bound to the remembrance or to the insistence. Just as their ancestors escaped the old country, so they can if they choose escape their old identities, the "inwardness" of their nativity. Kallen writes of the individual that "whatever else he changes, he cannot change his grandfather." [7] Perhaps not; but he can call his grandfather a "greenhorn," reject his customs and convictions, give up the family name, move to a new neighborhood, adopt a new "life-style."

He doesn't become a better American by doing these things (though that is sometimes his purpose), but he may become an American simply, an American and nothing else, freeing himself from the hyphenation that pluralists regard as universal on this side, though not on the other side, of the Atlantic Ocean. But, free from hyphenation, he seems also free from ethnicity: "American" is not one of the ethnic groups recognized in the United States census. Someone who is only an American is, so far as our bureaucrats are concerned, ethnically anonymous. He has a right, however, to his anonymity; that is part of what it means to be an American.

For a long time, British-Americans thought of themselves as Americans simply – and not anonymously: they constituted, so they would have said, a new ethnicity and a new nationality, into which all later immigrants would slowly assimilate. "Americanization" was a political program designed to make sure that assimilation would not be too slow a process, at a time, indeed, when it seemed not to be a recognizable *process* at all. But though there were individuals who did their best to assimilate, that is, to adopt, at least outwardly, the mores of British-Americans, that soon ceased to be a plausible path to

7 Kallen, *Culture and Democracy,* p. 94

an "American" future. The sheer number of non-British immigrants was too great. If there was to be a new nationality, it would have to come out of the melting pot, where the heat was applied equally to all groups, the earlier immigrants as well as the most recent ones. The anonymous American was, at the turn of the century, say, a place-holder for some unknown future person who would give cultural content to the name. Meanwhile, most Americans were hyphenated Americans, more or less friendly to their grandfathers, more or less committed to their manyness. And pluralism was an alternative political program designed to legitimate this manyness and to make it permanent—which would leave those individuals who were Americans and nothing else permanently anonymous, assimilated to a cultural nonidentity.

Citizens

But though these anonymous Americans were not better Americans for being or for having become anonymous, it is conceivable that they were, and are, better American *citizens*. If the manyness of America is cultural, its oneness is political, and it may be the case that men and women who are free from non-American cultures will commit themselves more fully to the American political system. Maybe cultural anonymity is the best possible grounding for American politics. From the beginning, of course, it has been the standard claim of British-Americans that their own culture is the best grounding. And there is obviously much to be said for that view. Despite the efforts of hyphenated Americans to describe liberal and democratic politics as a kind of United Way to which they have all made contributions, the genealogy of the American political system bears a close resemblance to the genealogy of the Sons and Daughters of the American Revolution – ethnic organizations if there ever were any![8] But this genealogy must also account for the flight across the Atlantic and the Revolutionary War. The parliamentary oligarchy of eighteenth-century Great Britain wasn't, after all, all that useful a model for America. When the ancestors of the Sons and Daughters described their political achievement as a "new order for the ages," they were celebrating a break with their own ethnic past almost as profound as that which later Americans were called upon to make. British-Americans who refused the break called themselves "Loyalists," but they were called disloyal by their opponents and treated even more harshly than hyphenated Americans from Germany, Russia, and Japan in later episodes of war and revolution.

Citizenship in the "new order" was not universally available, since blacks and women and Indians (Native Americans) were excluded, but it was never linked to a single nationality. "To be or to become an American," writes Philip Gleason, "a person did not have to be of any particular national, linguistic, religious, or ethnic background. All he had to do was to commit himself to the political ideology centered on the abstract ideals of liberty, equality, and republicanism."[9] These abstract ideals made for a politics separated not only from religion but from culture itself or, better, from all the particular forms in which religious and national culture was, and is, expressed – hence a politics "anonymous" in Kallen's sense. Anonymity suggests autonomy too, though I don't want to claim that American politics was not qualified in important ways by

8 See Kallen's account of how British-Americans were forced into ethnicity: *Culture and Democracy*, pp. 99f.

9 P. Gleason, "American Identity and Americanization," in *Harvard Encyclopedia*, p. 32.

British Protestantism, later by Irish Catholicism, later still by German, Italian, Polish, Jewish, African, and Hispanic religious commitments and political experience. But these qualifications never took what might be called a strong adjectival form, never became permanent or exclusive qualities of America's abstract politics and citizenship. The adjective "American" named, and still names, a politics that is relatively unqualified by religion or nationality or, alternatively, that is qualified by so many religions and nationalities as to be free from any one of them.

It is this freedom that makes it possible for America's oneness to encompass and protect its manyness. Nevertheless, the conflict between the one and the many is a pervasive feature of American life. Those Americans who attach great value to the oneness of citizenship and the centrality of political allegiance must seek to constrain the influence of cultural manyness; those who value the many must disparage the one. The conflict is evident from the earliest days of the republic, but I will begin my own account of it with the campaign to restrict immigration and naturalization in the 1850s. Commonly called "nativist" by historians, the campaign was probably closer in its politics to a Rousseauian republicanism.[10] Anti-Irish and anti-Catholic bigotry played a large part in mobilizing support for the American (or American Republican) party, popularly called the Know-Nothings; and the political style of the party, like that of contemporary abolitionists and free-soilers, displayed many of the characteristics of Protestant moralism. But in its self-presentation, it was above all repub-

10 On the complexities of "nativism," see John Higham, *Send These to Me: Jews and Other Immigrants in Urban America* (New York, Atheneum, 1975), pp. 102-115. For an account of the Know-Nothings different from mine, to which I am nonetheless indebted, see S.M. Lipset and Earl Raab, *The Politics of Unreason: Right-wing Extremism in America, 1790-1970*, (New York, Harper & Row, 1970), ch. 2.

lican, more concerned about the civic virtue of the new immigrants than about their ethnic lineages, its religious critique focused on the ostensible connection between Catholicism and tyranny. The legislative program of the Know-Nothings had to do largely with questions of citizenship at the national level and of public education at the local level. In Congress, where the party had 75 representatives (and perhaps another 45 sympathizers, out of a total of 234) at the peak of its strength in 1855, it seemed more committed to restricting the suffrage than to cutting off immigration. Some of its members would have barred "paupers" from entering the United States, and others would have required an oath of allegiance from all immigrants immediately upon landing. But their energy was directed mostly toward revising the naturalization laws.[11] It was not the elimination of manyness but its disenfranchisement that the Know-Nothings championed.

Something like this was probably the position of most American "nativists" until the last years of the nineteenth century. In 1845, when immigration rates were still fairly low, a group of "native Americans" meeting in Philadelphia declared that they would "kindly receive [all] persons who came to America, and give them every privilege except office and suffrage."[12] I would guess that the nativist view of American blacks was roughly similar. Most of the northern Know-Nothings (the party's greatest strength was in New England) were strongly opposed to slavery, but it did not follow from that opposition that they were prepared to welcome former slaves as fellow citizens. The logic of events led to citizenship, after a bloody war, and the Know-Nothings, by then loyal Republi-

11 Frank George Franklin, *The Legislative History of Naturalization in the United States* (New York: Arno Press, 1969), chs. 11-14.
12 *Ibid.*, p. 247.

cans, presumably supported that outcome. But the logic of republican principle, as they understood it, would have suggested some delay. Thus a resolution of the Massachusetts legislature in 1856 argued that "republican institutions were especially adapted to an educated and intelligent people, capable of *and accustomed to* self-government. Free institutions could be confined safely only to free men. . . "[13] The legislators went on to urge a twenty-one-year residence requirement for naturalization. Since it was intended that disenfranchised residents should nonetheless be full members of civil society, another piece of Know-Nothing legislation would have provided that any alien free white person (this came from a Mississippi senator) should be entitled after twelve months residence "to all the protection of the government, and [should] be allowed to inherit, and hold, and transmit real estate. . . in the same manner as though he were a citizen."[14]

Civil society, then, would include a great variety of ethnic and religious and perhaps even racial groups, but the members of these groups would acquire the "inestimable" good of citizenship only after a long period of practical education (but does one learn just by watching?) in democratic virtue. Meanwhile, their children would get a formal education. Despite their name, the Know-Nothings thought that citizenship was a subject about which a great deal had to be known. Some of them wanted to make attendance in public schools compulsory, but, faced with constitutional objections, they insisted only that no public funding should go to the support of parochial schools. It is worth emphasizing that the crucial principle here was not the separation of church and state. The

13 *Ibid.,* p. 293 (emphasis added).
14 *Ibid.*

Know-Nothing party did not oppose sabbatarian laws.[15] Its members believed that tax money should not be used to underwrite social manyness – not in the case of religion, obviously, but also not in the case of language and culture. Political identity, singular in form, would be publicly inculcated and defended; the plurality of social identities would have to be sustained in private.

I don't doubt that most nativists hoped that plurality would not, in fact, be sustained. They had ideas, if not sociological theories, about the connection of politics and culture – specifically, as I have said, republican politics and British Protestant culture. I don't mean to underestimate the centrality of these ideas: this was presumably the knowledge that the Know-Nothings were concealing when they claimed to know nothing. Nonetheless, the logic of their position, as of any "American" republican position, pressed toward the creation of a politics independent of all the ethnicities and religions of civil society. Otherwise too many people would be excluded; the political world would look too much like Old England and not at all like the "new order of the ages," not at all like "America." Nor could American nativists challenge ethnic and religious pluralism directly, for both were protected (as the parochial schools were protected) by the constitution to which they claimed a passionate attachment. They could only insist that passionate attachment should be the mark of all citizens – and set forth the usual arguments against the seriousness of love at first sight and in favor of long engagements. They wanted what Rousseau wanted: that citizens should find the greater share of their happiness in public (political) rather than in private (social) activities.[16] And they were prepared

15 Lipset and Raab, *Politics of Unreason*, p. 46.
16 Jean-Jacques Rousseau, *The Social Contract*, trans. G. D. H. Cole (New York: Dutton,

to deny citizenship to men and women who seemed to them especially unlikely to do that.

No doubt, again, public happiness came easily to the nativists because they felt so entirely at home in American public life. But we should not be too quick to attribute this feeling to the carry-over of ethnic consciousness into the political sphere. For American politics in the 1850s was already so open, egalitarian, and democratic (relative to European politics) that almost anyone could feel at home in it. Precisely because the United States was no one's *national* home, its politics was universally accessible. All that was necessary in principle was ideological commitment, in practice, a good line of talk. The Irish did very well and demonstrated as conclusively as one could wish that "British" and "Protestant" were not necessary adjectives for American politics. They attached to the many, not to the one.

For this reason, the symbols and ceremonies of American citizenship could not be drawn from the political culture or history of British-Americans. Our Congress is not a Commons; Guy Fawkes Day is not an American holiday; the Magna Carta has never been one of our sacred texts. American symbols and ceremonies are culturally anonymous, invented rather than inherited, voluntaristic in style, narrowly political in content: the flag, the Pledge, the Fourth, the Constitution. It is entirely appropriate that the Know-Nothing party had its origin in the Secret Society of the Star-Spangled Banner. And it is entirely understandable that the flag and the Pledge continue, even today to figure largely in political debate. With what reverence should the flag be treated? On what occasions must it be saluted? Should we require school children to re-

---

16 *con.* 1950), bk. III, ch. 15, p. 93.

cite the Pledge, teachers to lead the recitation? Questions like these are the tests of a political commitment that can't be assumed, because it isn't undergirded by the cultural and religious commonalities that make for mutual trust. The flag and the Pledge are, as it were, all we have. One could suggest, of course, alternative and more practical tests of loyalty – responsible participation in political life, for example. But the real historical alternative is the test proposed by the cultural pluralists: one proves one's Americanism, in their view, by living in peace with all the other "Americans," that is, by agreeing to respect social manyness rather than by pledging allegiance to the "one and indivisible" republic. And pluralists are led on by the logic of this argument to suggest that citizenship is something less than an "inestimable" good.

Hyphenated Americans

Good it certainly was to be an American citizen. Horace Kallen was prepared to call citizenship a "great vocation," but he clearly did not believe (in the 1910s and '20s, when he wrote his classic essays on cultural pluralism) that one could make a life there. Politics was a necessary, but not a spiritually sustaining activity. It was best understood in instrumental terms; it had to do with the arrangements that made it possible for groups of citizens to "realize and protect" their diverse cultures and "attain the excellence appropriate to their kind."[17] These arrangements, Kallen thought, had to be democratic, and democracy required citizens of a certain sort – autonomous, self-disciplined, capable of cooperation and com-

---

17 Kallen, *Culture and Democracy*, p. 61

promise. "Americanization" was entirely legitimate insofar as it aimed to develop these qualities; they made up Kallen's version of civic virtue, and he was willing to say that they should be common to all Americans. But, curiously perhaps, they did not touch the deeper self. "The common city-life, which depends upon like-mindedness, is not inward, corporate, and inevitable, but external, inarticulate, and incidental. . . not the expression of a homogeneity of heritage, mentality, and interest."[18]

Hence Kallen's program: assimilation "in matters economic and political," dissimilation "in cultural consciousness."[19] The hyphen joined these two processes in one person, so that a Jewish-American (like Kallen) was similar to other Americans in his economic and political activity, but similar only to other Jews at the deeper level of culture.[20] It is clear that Kallen's "hyphenates," whose spiritual life is located so emphatically to the left of the hyphen, cannot derive the greater part of their happiness from their citizenship. Nor, in a sense, should they, since culture, for the cultural pluralists, is far more important than politics and promises a more complete satisfaction. Pluralists, it seems, do not make good republicans – for the same reason that republicans, Rousseau the classic example, do not make good pluralists. The two attend to different sorts of goods.

Kallen's hyphenated Americans can be attentive and conscientious citizens, but on a liberal, not a republican model. This

18 *Ibid.*, p. 78.
19 *Ibid.*, pp. 114-115.
20 It is interesting that both nativists and pluralists wanted to keep the market free of ethnic and religious considerations. The Know-Nothings, since they thought that democratic politics was best served by British ethnicity and Protestant religion, set the market firmly within civil society, allowing full market rights even to new and Catholic immigrants. Kallen, by contrast, since he understands civil society as a world of ethnic and religious groups, assimilates the market to the universality of the political sphere, the "common city-life."

means two things. First, the various ethnic and religious groups can intervene in political life only in order to defend themselves and advance their common interests – as in the case of the NAACP or the Anti-Defamation League – but not in order to impose their culture or their values. They have to recognize that the state is anonymous (or, in the language of contemporary political theorists, neutral) at least in this sense: that it can't take on the character or the name of any of the groups that it includes. It isn't a nation-state of a particular kind and it isn't a Christian republic. Second, the primary political commitment of individual citizens is to protect their protection, to uphold the democratic framework within which they pursue their more substantive activities. This commitment is consistent with feelings of gratitude, loyalty, even patriotism of a certain sort, but it doesn't make for fellowship. There is indeed *union* in politics (and economics) but union of a sort that precludes intimacy. "The political and economic life of the commonwealth," writes Kallen, "is a single unit and serves as the foundation and background for the realization of the distinctive individuality of each *nation*."[21] Here pluralism is straightforwardly opposed to republicanism: politics offers neither self-realization nor communion. All intensity lies, or should lie, elsewhere.

Kallen believes, of course, that this "elsewhere" actually exists; his is not a utopian vision; it's not a case of "elsewhere, perhaps." The "organic groups" that make up Kallen's America appear in public life as interest groups only, organized for the pursuit of material and social goods that are universally desired but sometimes in short supply and often unfairly distributed. That is the only appearance countenanced by a liberal and democratic political system. But behind it, concealed

21 Kallen, *Culture and Democracy*, p. 124.

from public view, lies the true significance of ethnicity or religion: "It is the center at which [the individual] stands, the point of his most intimate social relations, therefore of his intensest emotional life."[22] I am inclined to say that this is too radical a view of ethnic and religious identification, since it seems to rule out moral conflicts in which the individual's emotions are enlisted, as it were, on both sides. But Kallen's more important point is simply that there is space and opportunity *elsewhere* for the emotional satisfactions that politics can't (or shouldn't) provide. And because individuals really do find this satisfaction, the groups within which it is found are permanently sustainable: they won't melt down, not, at least, in any ordinary (noncoercive) social process. Perhaps they can be repressed, if the repression is sufficiently savage; even then, they will win out in the end.

Kallen wasn't entirely unaware of the powerful forces making for cultural meltdown, even without repression. He has some strong lines on the effectiveness of the mass media – though he knew these only in their infancy and at a time when newspapers were still a highly localized medium and the foreign-language press flourished. In his analysis and critique of the pressure to conform, he anticipated what became by the 1950s a distinctively American genre of social criticism. It isn't always clear whether he sees pluralism as a safeguard against or an antidote for the conformity of ethnic-Americans to that spiritless "Americanism" he so much disliked, a dull protective coloring that destroys all inner brightness. In any case, he is sure that inner brightness will survive, "for Nature is naturally pluralistic; her unities are eventual, not primary."[23] Eventually, he means, the American union will prove to

22 *Ibid.*, p. 200.
23 *Ibid.*, p. 179.

be a matter of "mutual accommodation," leaving intact the primacy of ethnic and religious identity. In the years since Kallen wrote, this view has gathered a great deal of ideological, but much less of empirical, support. "Pluralist principles . . . have been on the ascendancy," writes a contemporary critic of pluralism, "precisely at a time when ethnic differences have been on the wane."[24] What if the "excellence" appropriate to our "kind" is, simply, an American excellence? Not necessarily civic virtue of the sort favored by nativists, republicans, and contemporary communitarians, but nonetheless some local color, a brightness of our own?

Peripheral Distance

This local color is most visible, I suppose, in popular culture—which is entirely appropriate in the case of the world's first mass democracy. Consider, for example, the movie *American in Paris,* where the hero is an American simply and not at all an Irish- or German- or Jewish-American. Do we drop our hyphens when we travel abroad? But what are we, then, without them? We carry with us cultural artifacts of a quite specific sort: *"une danse americaine,"* Gene Kelly tells the French children as he begins to tap dance. What else could he call it, this melted-down combination of Northern English clog dancing, the Irish jig and reel, and African rhythmic foot stamping, to which had been added, by Kelly's time, the influence of the French and Russian ballet? Creativity of this sort is both explained and celebrated by those writers and thinkers, heroes of the higher culture, that we are likely to recognize as dis-

24 Stephen Steinberg, *The Ethnic Myth: Race, Ethnicity, and Class in America* (Boston, Beacon Press, 1981), p. 254.

tinctively American: thus Emerson's defense of the experimental life (I am not sure, though, that he would have admired tap dancing), or Whitman's democratic inclusiveness, or the pragmatism of Peirce and James.

"An American nationality," writes Gleason, "does in fact exist."[25] Not just a political status, backed up by a set of political symbols and ceremonies, but a full-blooded nationality, reflecting a history and a culture – exactly like all the other nationalities from which Americans have been, and continue to be, recruited. The ongoing immigration makes it difficult to see the real success of Americanization in creating distinctive types, characters, styles, artifacts of all sorts which, were Gene Kelly to display them to his Parisian neighbors, they would rightly recognize as "American." More important, Americans recognize one another, take pride in the things that fellow Americans have made and done, identify with the national community. So, while there no doubt are people plausibly called Italian-Americans or Swedish-Americans, spiritual (as well as political) life – this is Gleason's view – is lived largely to the right of the hyphen: contrasted with real Italians and real Swedes, these are real Americans.

This view seems to me both right and wrong. It is right in its denial of Kallen's account of America as an anonymous nation of named nationalities. It is wrong in its insistence that America is a nation like all the others. But the truth does not lie, where we might naturally be led to look for it, somewhere between this rightness and this wrongness – as if we could locate America at some precise point along the continuum that stretches from the many to the one. I want to take the advice of that American song, another product of the

25 Gleason, "American Identity," p. 56.

popular culture, which tells us: "Don't mess with mister in-between."[26] If there are cultural artifacts, songs and dances, styles of life and even philosophies, that are distinctively American, there is also an idea of America that is itself distinct, incorporating oneness and manyness in a "new order" that may or may not be "for the ages" but that is certainly for us, here and now.

The cultural pluralists come closer to getting the new order right than do the nativists and the nationalists and the American communitarians. Nonetheless, there is a nation and a national community and, by now, a very large number of native Americans. Even first- and second-generation Americans, as Gleason points out, have graves to visit and homes and neighborhoods to remember *in this country,* on this side of whatever waters their ancestors crossed to get here.[27] What is distinctive about the nationality of these Americans is not its insubstantial character – substance is quickly acquired – but its nonexclusive character. Remembering the God of the Hebrew Bible, I want to argue that America is not a jealous nation. In this sense, at least, it is different from most of the others.

Consider, for example, a classic moment in the ethnic history of France: the debate over the emancipation of the Jews in 1790 and '91. It is not, by any means, a critical moment; there were fewer than 35,000 Jews in revolutionary France, only 500 in Paris. The Jews were not economically powerful or politically significant or even intellectually engaged in French life (all that could come only after emancipation). But the debate nonetheless was long and serious, for it dealt with the meaning of citizenship and nationality. When the Constituent Assembly voted for full emancipation in September

26 The song is "Accentuate the Positive," which is probably what I am doing here.
27 Gleason, "American Identity," p. 56

1791, its position was summed up by Clermont-Tonnerre, a deputy of the Center, in a famous sentence: "One must refuse everything to the Jews as a nation, and give everything to the Jews as individuals. . . It would be repugnant to have. . . a nation within a nation."[28] The Assembly's vote led to the disestablishment of Jewish corporate existence in France, which had been sanctioned and protected by the monarchy. "Refusing everything to the Jews as a nation" meant withdrawing the sanction, denying the protection. Henceforth Jewish communities would be voluntary associations, and individual Jews would have rights against the community as well as against the state: Clermont-Tonnerre was a good liberal.

But the Assembly debate also suggests that most of the deputies favoring emancipation would not have looked with favor even on the voluntary associations of the Jews, insofar as these reflected national sensibility or cultural difference. The future Girondin leader Brissot, defending emancipation, predicted that Jews who became French citizens would "lose their particular characteristics." I suspect that he could hardly imagine a greater triumph of French *civisme* than this – as if the secular Second Coming, like the religious version, awaited only the conversion of the Jews. Brissot thought the day was near: "Their eligibility [for citizenship] will regenerate them."[29] Jews could be good citizens only insofar as they were regenerated, which meant, in effect, that they could be good citizens only insofar as they became French. (They must, after all, have some "particular characteristics," and if not their own, then whose?) Their emancipators had, no doubt, a generous view

28 Quoted in Gary Kates, "Jews into Frenchmen: Nationality and Representation in Revolutionary France," *Social Research* 56 (Spring 1989): 229. See also the discussion in Arthur Hertzberg, *The French Enlightenment and the Jews: The Origins of Modern Anti-Semitism* (New York: Schocken, 1970), pp. 360-362.

29 Kates, "Jews into Frenchmen," p. 229.

of their capacity to do that but would not have been generous in the face of resistance (from the Jews or from any other of the corporate groups of the old regime). The price of emancipation was assimilation.

This has been the French view of citizenship ever since. Though they have often been generous in granting the exalted status of citizen to foreigners, the successive republics have been suspicious of any form of ethnic pluralism. Each republic really has been "one and indivisible," and it has been established, as Rousseau thought it should be, on a strong national oneness. Oneness all the way down is, on this view, the only guarantee that the general will and the common good will triumph in French politics.

America is very different, and not only because of the eclipse of republicanism in the early nineteenth century. Indeed, republicanism has had a kind of afterlife as one of the legitimating ideologies of American politics. The Minute Man is a republican image of embodied citizenship. Reverence for the flag is a form of republican piety. The Pledge of Allegiance is a republican oath. But emphasis on this sort of thing reflects social disunity rather than unity; it is a straining after oneness where oneness doesn't exist. In fact, America has been, with severe but episodic exceptions, remarkably tolerant of ethnic pluralism (far less so of racial pluralism).[30] I don't want to underestimate the human difficulties of adapting even to a hyphenated Americanism, nor to deny the bigotry and discrimination that particular groups have encountered. But tolerance has been the cultural norm.

Perhaps an immigrant society has no choice; tolerance is a way of muddling through when any alternative policy would

---

30 The current demand of (some) black Americans that they be called African-Americans represents an attempt to adapt themselves to the ethnic paradigm—imitating, perhaps, the

be violent and dangerous. But I would argue that we have, mostly, made the best of this necessity, so that the virtues of toleration, in principle though by no means always in practice, have supplanted the singlemindedness of republican citizenship. We have made our peace with the "particular characteristics" of all the immigrant groups (though not, again, of all the racial groups) and have come to regard American nationality as an addition to rather than a replacement for ethnic consciousness. The hyphen works, when it is working, more like a plus sign. "American," then, is a name indeed, but unlike "French" or "German" or "Italian" or "Korean" or "Japanese" or "Cambodian," it can serve as a second name. And as in those modern marriages where two patronymics are joined, neither the first nor the second name is dominant: here the hyphen works more like a sign of equality.

We might go further than this: in the case of hyphenated Americans, it doesn't matter whether the first or the second name is dominant. We insist, most of the time, that the "particular characteristics" associated with the first name be sustained, as the Know-Nothings urged, without state help – and perhaps they will prove unsustainable on those terms. Still, an ethnic-American is someone who can, in principle, live his spiritual life as he chooses, *on either side of the hyphen*. In this sense, American citizenship is indeed anonymous, for it doesn't require a full commitment to American (or to any other) nationality. The distinctive national culture that Amer-

---

30 *con.* relative success of various Asian-American groups in a similar adaptation. But names are no guarantees; nor does antinativist pluralism provide sufficient protection against what is all too often an *ethnic*-American racism. It has been argued that this racism is the necessary precondition of hyphenated ethnicity: the inclusion of successive waves of ethnic immigrants is possible only because of the permanent exclusion of black Americans. But I don't know what evidence would demonstrate *necessity* here. I am inclined to reject the metaphysical belief that all inclusion entails exclusion. A historical and empirical account of the place of blacks in the "system" of American pluralism would require another essay, a different book.

icans have created doesn't underpin, it exists alongside of, American politics. It follows, then, that the people I earlier called Americans simply, Americans and nothing else, have in fact a more complicated existence than those terms suggest. They are American-Americans, one more group of hyphenates (not quite the same as all the others), and one can imagine them attending to the cultural aspects of their Americanism and refusing the political commitment that republican ideology demands. They might still be good or bad citizens. And similarly, Orthodox Jews as well as secular (regenerate) Jews, Protestant fundamentalists as well as liberal Protestants, Irish republicans as well as Irish Democrats, black nationalists as well as black integrationists – all these can be good or bad citizens, given the American (liberal rather than republican) understanding of citizenship.

One step more is required before we have fully understood this strange America: it is not the case that Irish-Americans, say, are culturally Irish and politically American, as the pluralists claim (and as I have been assuming thus far for the sake of the argument). Rather, they are culturally Irish-American and politically Irish-American. Their culture has been significantly influenced by American culture; their politics is still, both in style and substance, significantly ethnic. With them, and with every ethnic and religious group except the American-Americans, hyphenation is doubled. It remains true, however, that what all the groups have in common is most importantly their citizenship and what most differentiates them, insofar as they are still differentiated, is their culture. Hence the alternation in American life of patriotic fevers and ethnic revivals, the first expressing a desire to heighten the commonality, the second a desire to reaffirm the difference.

At both ends of this peculiarly American alternation, the good that is defended is also exaggerated and distorted, so that pluralism itself is threatened by the sentiments it generates. The patriotic fevers are the symptoms of a republican pathology. At issue here is the all-important ideological commitment that, as Gleason says, is the sole prerequisite of American citizenship. Since citizenship isn't guaranteed by oneness all the way down, patriots or superpatriots seek to guarantee it by loyalty oaths and campaigns against "un-American" activities. The Know-Nothing party having failed to restrict naturalization, they resort instead to political purges and deportations. Ethnic revivals are less militant and less cruel, though not without their own pathology. What is at issue here is communal pride and power – a demand for political recognition without assimilation, an assertion of interest-group politics against republican ideology, an effort to distinguish this group (one's own) from all the others. American patriotism is always strained and nervous because hyphenation makes indeed for dual loyalty but seems, at the same time, entirely American. Ethnic revivalism is also strained and nervous, because the hyphenates are already Americans, on both sides of the hyphen.

In these circumstances, republicanism is a mirage, and American nationalism or communitarianism is not a plausible option; it doesn't reach to our complexity. A certain sort of communitarianism is available to each of the hyphenate groups – except, it would seem, the American-Americans, whose community, if it existed, would deny the Americanism of all the others. So Horace Kallen is best described as a Jewish (-American) communitarian and a (Jewish-) American liberal, and this kind of coexistence, more widely realized, would constitute the pattern he called cultural pluralism. But the different ethnic and religious communities are all of them far more precarious than he thought, for they have, in a liberal political system, no corporate form or legal structure or coercive power. And, without these supports, the "inherited organic set" seems to dissipate – the population lacks cohesion, cultural life lacks coherence. The resulting "groups" are best conceived, John Higham suggests, as a core of activists and believers and an expanding periphery of passive members or followers, lost, as it were, in a wider America.[31] At the core, the left side of the (double) hyphen is stronger; along the periphery, the right side is stronger, though never fully dominant. Americans choose, as it were, their own location; and it appears that a growing number of them are choosing to fade into the peripheral distances. They become American-Americans, though without much passion invested in the becoming. But if the core doesn't hold, it also doesn't disappear; it is still capable of periodic revival.

At the same time, continued large-scale immigration reproduces a Kallenesque pluralism, creating new groups of hyphenate Americans and encouraging revivalism among activists and believers in the old groups. America is still a radically unfinished society, and for now, at least, it makes sense to say that this unfinishedness is one of its distinctive features. The country has a political center, but it remains in every other sense decentered. More than this, the political center, despite occasional patriotic fevers, doesn't work against decentering elsewhere. It neither requires nor demands the kind of commitment that would put the legitimacy of ethnic or religious identification in doubt. It doesn't aim at a finished or fully coherent Americanism. Indeed, American politics, itself plu-

---

31 Higham, *Send These to Me*, p. 242.

ralist in character, *needs* a certain sort of incoherence. A radical program of Americanization would really be unAmerican. It isn't inconceivable that America will one day become an American nation-state, the many giving way to the one, but that is not what it is now; nor is that its destiny. America has no singular national destiny – and to be an "American" is, finally, to know that and to be more or less content with it.

PLURALISM: A
POLITICAL PERSPECTIVE

Democracy and Nationalism

Most political theorists, from the time of the Greeks onward, have assumed the national or ethnic homogeneity of the communities about which they wrote. Prior to the work of Rousseau, theory was never explicitly nationalist, but the assumption of a common language, history, or religion under- lay most of what was said about political practices and insti- tutions. Hence, the only empire systematically defended in the great tradition of political theory was the Christian empire of the Middle Ages: one religious communion, it was argued, made one political community. The religiously mixed empires of ancient and modern times, by contrast, had no theoretical defenders, only publicists and apologists. Political thinking has been dominated by the Greece of Pericles, not of Alexander; by republican Rome, not the Roman empire; by Venice and Holland, not the Europe of the Hapsburgs. Even liberal writers, ready enough to acknowledge a plurality of interests, were strikingly unready for a plurality of cultures. One people made one state. The argument of the authors of *The Federalist Papers* may be taken here to sum up a long tra- dition of thought. The Americans, John Jay wrote, were a people "descended from the same ancestors, speaking the same language, professing the same religion, attached to the same principles of government, very similar in their manners and customs." Surely a "band of brethren" so united "should never be split into a number of unsocial, jealous, and alien sovereignties."

Jay's description was only very roughly true of America in 1787, and clearly the maxim *One people, one state* has, throughout human history, been honored most often in the breach. Most often, brethren have been divided among alien sovereignties and forced to coexist with strangers under an alien sovereign. National and ethnic pluralism has been the rule, not the exception. The theoretical preference for cultural unity existed for centuries alongside dynastic and imperial institutions that made for disunity. Only in the late 18th and 19th centuries was the old assumption of homogeneity, reinforced by new democratic commitments, transformed into a practical demand for separation and independence. Underlying that demand were two powerful ideas: first, that free government was only possible under conditions of cultural unity; second, that free individuals would choose if they could to live with their own kind, that is, to join political sovereignty to national or ethnic community. No doubt these ideas could be challenged. Marx and his followers emphatically denied that they were true, arguing that conceptions of "kind" were ultimately based on class rather than ethnic distinctions. But the two ideas had the support of a long intellectual tradition, and they happily supported one another. They suggested that democracy and self-determination led to the same political arrangements that their effective exercise required: the replacement of empires by national states.

In practice, this replacement took two very different forms. The new nationalist politics was first of all expressed in the demand for the unification of peoples divided – as were the Germans, Italians, and Slavs – among the old empires and a variety of petty principalities. Nationalist leaders aimed initially at large states and at a broad (pan-German or pan-Slavic) definition of cultural homogeneity. Yugoslavia and Czechoslovakia were products of this first nationalism which, though it entailed the breakup of empires, was still a politics of composition, not of division. The Zionist "ingathering" of Jews from Europe and the Orient has the same character. Roughly similar groups were to be welded together, on the model of the prenationalist unifications of France and Britain.

This early nation-building was hardly a failure, but the clear tendency of nationalism more recently has been to challenge not only the old empires, especially the colonial empires, but also the composite nation-states. Neither the oldest states (France, Britain) nor the newest (Pakistan, Nigeria) have been safe from such challenges. Secession rather than unification is the current theme. International society today is marked by the proliferation of states so that "the majority of the members of the U.N.," as Eric Hobsbawm has written, "is soon likely to consist of the late-twentieth-century (republican) equivalents of Saxe-Coburg-Gotha and Schwarzburg-Sonderhausen." Important transformations of the world economy have opened the way for this process: the rules of viability have radically changed since the 19th century. The process also represents an extraordinary triumph for the principle of self-determination – with the collective self increasingly defined in ways that reflect the actual diversity of humankind.

Confronted with this diversity, every putative nation-state is revealed as an ancient or modern composition. Self-determination looks to be a principle of endless applicability, and the appearance of new states a process of indefinite duration. If the process is to be cut short, it will not be by denying the principle – for it appears today politically undeniable – but rather by administering it in moderate doses. Thus autonomy may be an alternative to independence, loosening the bonds of the composite state a way to avoid their fracture. Instead of sovereignty, national and ethnic groups may opt for decentralization, devolution, and federalism; these are not incompatible with self-determination, and they may be especially appropriate for groups of people who share some but not all of the characteristics of a distinct historical community and who retain a strong territorial base. Whether composite states can survive as federations is by no means certain, but it is unlikely that they can survive in any other way – not at least, if they remain committed (even if only formally) to democratic government or to some sort of social egalitarianism.

Democracy and equality have proven to be the great solvents. In the old empires, the elites of conquered nations tended to assimilate to the dominant culture. They sent their children to be educated by their conquerors; they learned an alien language; they came to see their own culture as parochial and inferior. But ordinary men and women did not assimilate, and when they were mobilized, first for economic and then for political activity, they turned out to have deep national and ethnic loyalties. Mobilization made for conflict, not only with the dominant groups, but also with other submerged peoples. For centuries, perhaps, different nations had lived in peace, side by side, under imperial rule. Now that they had to rule themselves, they found that they could do so (peacefully) only among themselves, adjusting political lines to cultural boundaries.

So the assumptions of the theoretical tradition have proven true. Self-government has tended to produce relatively homogeneous communities and has been fully successful only within such communities. The great exception to this rule is the United States. At the same time, the Marxist argument, the most significant challenge to traditional wisdom, has proven wrong. Nowhere have class loyalties overridden the commitment to national and ethnic groups. The Soviet Union before its collapse resembled nothing so much as the empire of the Romanovs: a multinational state held together chiefly by force. Conceivably, if the "national question" were ever solved, if the existence and continued development of historical communities were guaranteed (as Lenin argued they should be), new patterns of alliance and cooperation might emerge. But for the moment, it must be said that politics follows nationality, wherever politics is free. Pluralism in the strong sense – *One state, many peoples* – is possible only under tyrannical regimes.

American Exceptionalism

Except in the United States. Here too, of course, there are conquered and incorporated peoples – Indian tribes, Mexicans – who stood in the path of American expansion, and there are forcibly transported peoples – the blacks – brought to this country as slaves and subjected to a harsh and continuous repression. But the pluralist system within which these groups have only recently begun to organize and act is not primarily the product of their experience. Today, the United States can only be understood as a multiracial society. But the minority races were politically impotent and socially invisible during much of the time when American pluralism was taking shape — and the shape it took was not determined by their presence or by their repression.

In contrast to the Old World, where pluralism had its origins in conquest and dynastic alliance, pluralism in the New World originated in individual and familial migration. The largest part of the U.S. population was formed by the addition of individuals, one by one, filtered through the great port cities. Though the boundaries of the new country, like those of every other country, were determined by war and diplomacy, it was immigration that determined the character of its inhabitants — and falsified John Jay's account of their unity. The United States was not an empire; its pluralism was that of an immigrant society, and that means that nationality and ethnicity never acquired a stable territorial base. Different peoples gathered in different parts of the country, but they did so by individual choice, clustering for company, with no special tie to the land on which they lived. The Old World call for self-determination had no resonance here: the immigrants (except for the black slaves) had come voluntarily and did not have to be forced to stay (indeed, many of them returned home each year), nor did groups of immigrants have any basis for or any reason for secession. The only significant secessionist movement in U.S. history, though it involved a region with a distinct culture, did not draw upon nationalist passions of the sort that have figured in European wars. >>

But if the immigrants became Americans one by one as they arrived and settled, they did so only in a political sense: they

58

became U.S. citizens. In other respects, culturally, religiously, even for a time linguistically, they remained Germans and Swedes, Poles, Jews, and Italians. With regard to the first immigrants, the Anglo-Americans, politics still followed nationality. Because they were one people, they made one state. But with the newer immigrants, the process was reversed. Because they were citizens of one state – so it was commonly thought – they would become one people. Nationality would follow politics, as it presumably had in earlier times, when the peoples of the modern world were first formed. For a while, however, perhaps for a long while, the United States would be a country composed of many peoples, sharing residence and citizenship only, without a common history or culture.

In such circumstances, the only emotion that made for unity was patriotism. Hence the efforts of the late nineteenth and early twentieth centuries to intensify patriotic feeling, to make a religion out of citizenship. "The voting booth is the temple of American institutions," Supreme Court Justice David Brewer wrote in 1900. "No single tribe or family is chosen to watch the sacred fires burning on its altars. . . Each of us is a priest." The rise of ethnic political machines and block voting, however, must have made the temple seem disturbingly like a sectarian conventicle. Few people believed politics to be a sufficient ground for national unity. Patriotism was essentially a holding action while the country waited for the stronger solidarity of nationalism. Whether the process of Americanization was described as a gradual assimilation to Anglo-American culture or as the creation of an essentially new culture in the crucible of citizenship, its outcome was thought to be both necessary and inevitable: the immigrants would one day constitute a single people. This was the deeper meaning that the slogan *From many, one (E pluribus unum)* took on in the context of mass immigration. The only alternatives, as the history of the Old World taught, were divisiveness, turmoil, and repression.

The fear of divisiveness, or simply of difference, periodically generated outbursts of anti-immigrant feeling among the first immigrants and their descendants. Restraint of all further immigration was one goal of the "nativist" campaigns of the early 1900s; the second goal was a more rapid Americanization of the "foreigners" already here. But what did Americanization entail? Many of the foreigners were already naturalized citizens. Now they were to be naturalized again, not politically but culturally. It is worth distinguishing this second naturalization from superficially similar campaigns in the old European empires. Russification, for example, was also a cultural program, but it was aimed at intact and rooted communities, at nations that, with the exception of the Jews, were established on lands they had occupied for many centuries. None of the peoples who were to be Russified could have been trusted with citizenship in a free Russia. Given the chance, they would have opted for secession and independence. That was why Russification was so critical: political means were required to overcome national differences. And the use of those means produced the predictable democratic response that politics should follow nationality, not oppose it. In the United States, by contrast, Americanization was aimed at peoples far more susceptible to cultural change, for they were not only uprooted; they had uprooted themselves. Whatever the pressures that had driven them to the New World, they had chosen to come, while others like themselves, in their own families, had chosen to remain. And as a reward for their choice, the immigrants had been offered citizenship, a gift that many eagerly accepted. Though nativists feared or pretended to fear the politics of the newcomers, the fact is that the men and women who were to be Americanized were already, many of them, patriotic Americans.

Because of these differences, the response of the immigrants to cultural naturalization was very different from that of their counterparts in the Old World. They were in many cases acquiescent, ready to make themselves over, even as the nativists asked. This was especially true in the area of language: there has been no longterm or successful effort to maintain the original language of the newcomers as anything more than a second language in the United States. The vitality of Spanish in the Southwest today, though it probably results from the continued large-scale influx of Mexican immigrants, suggests a possible exception to this rule. If these immigrants do not distribute themselves around the country, as other groups have done, a state like New Mexico might provide the first arena for sustained linguistic conflict in the United States. Until now, however, in a country where many languages are spoken, there has been remarkably little conflict. English is and has always been acknowledged as the public language of the American republic, and no one has tried to make any other language the basis for regional autonomy or secession. When the immigrants did resist Americanization, struggling to hold on to old identities and old customs, their resistance took a new form. It was not a demand that politics follow nationality, but rather that politics be separated from nationality – as it was already separated from religion. It was not a demand for national liberation, but for ethnic pluralism.

MICHAEL WALZER

The Practice of Pluralism

As a general intellectual tendency, pluralism in the early twentieth century was above all a reaction against the doctrine of sovereignty. In its different forms – syndicalist, guild socialist, regionalist, autonomist – it was directed against the growing power and the far-reaching claims of the modern state. But ethnic pluralism as it developed in the United States cannot plausibly be characterized as an antistate ideology. Its advocates did not challenge the authority of the federal government; they did not defend states' rights; they were not drawn to any of the forms of European corporatism. Their central assertion was that U.S. politics, as it was, did not require cultural homogeneity; it rested securely enough on democratic citizenship. What had previously been understood as a temporary condition was now described as if it might be permanent. The United States was, and could safely remain, a country composed of many peoples, a "nation of nationalities," as Horace Kallen called it. Indeed, this was the destiny of America: to maintain the diversity of the Old World in a single state, without persecution or repression. Not only *From many, one,* but also *Within one, many.*

Marxism was the first major challenge to the traditional argument for national homogeneity; ethnic pluralism is the second. Although the early pluralists were by no means radicals, and never advocated social transformation, there is a certain sense in which their denial of conventional wisdom goes deeper than that of the Marxists. For the Marxist argument suggests that the future socialist state (before it withers away) will rest upon the firm base of proletarian unity. And like each previous ruling class, the proletariat is expected to produce a hegemonic culture, of which political life would be merely one expression. Pluralists, on the other hand, imagined a state unsupported by either unity or hegemony. No doubt, they were naive not to recognize the existence of a single economic system and then of a culture reflecting dominant economic values. But their argument is far-reaching and important even if it is taken to hold only that in addition to this common culture, overlaying it, radically diversifying its impact, there is a world of ethnic multiplicity. The effect on the theory of the state is roughly the same with or without the economic understanding: politics must still create the (national) unity it was once thought merely to mirror. And it must create unity without denying or repressing multiplicity.

The early pluralist writers – theorists like Horace Kallen and Randolph Bourne, popularizers like Louis Adamic – did not produce a fully satisfying account of this creative process or of the ultimately desirable relation between the political one and the cultural many. Their arguments rarely advanced much beyond glowing description and polemical assertion. Drawing heavily upon nineteenth-century romanticism, they insisted upon the intrinsic value of human difference and, more plausibly and importantly, upon the deep need of human beings for historically and communally structured forms of life. Every kind of regimentation, every kind of uniformity was alien to them. They were the self-appointed guardians of a society of groups, a society resting upon stable families (despite the disruptions of the immigrant experience), tied into, bearing, and transmitting powerful cultural traditions. At the same time, their politics was little more than an unexamined liberalism. Freedom for individuals, they were certain, was all that was necessary to uphold group identification and ethnic flourishing. They had surprisingly little to say about how the different groups were to be held together in a single political order, what citizenship might mean in a pluralist society, whether state power should ever be used on behalf of groups, or what social activities should be assigned to or left to groups. The practical meaning of ethnic pluralism has been hammered out, is still being hammered out, in the various arenas of political and social life. Little theoretical justification exists for any particular outcome.

The best way to understand pluralism, then, is to look at what its protagonists have done or tried to do. Ethnic self-assertion in the United States has been the functional equivalent of national liberation in other parts of the world. What are the actual functions that it serves? There are three that seem critically important. First of all, the defense of ethnicity against cultural naturalization: Kallen's pluralism, worked out in a period of heightened nativist agitation and political persecution, is primarily concerned with upholding the right of the new immigrants, as individuals, to form themselves into cultural communities and maintain their foreign ways. Kallen joins the early-twentieth-century American *kulturkampf* as the advocate of cultural permissiveness. Train citizens, but leave nationality alone! The argument, so far as it is developed, is largely negative in character, and so it fits easily into the liberal paradigm. But Kallen is convinced that the chief product of a liberal society will not be individual selfhood but collective identity. Here surely he was right, or at least partly right. How many private wars, parallel to his intellectual campaign, have been fought on behalf of such identities – in schools, bureaucracies, corporations – against the pressures of Americanization! Most often, when individual men and women insist on "being themselves," they are in fact defending a self they share with others. Sometimes, of course, they succumb and learn to conform to standardized versions of New World behavior. Or they wait, frightened and passive, for organizational support: a league against defamation, a committee for advancement, and so on. When such organizations go to work, the pluralist form of the struggle is plain to see, even if legal and moral arguments continue to focus on individual rights.

The second function of ethnic assertiveness is more positive in character: the celebration of this or that identity. Celebration is critical to every national and ethnic movement because both foreign conquest and immigration to foreign lands work, though in different ways, to undermine communal confidence. Immigration involves a conscious rejection of the old country and then, often, of oneself as a product of the old country. A new land requires a new life, new ways of life. But in learning the new ways, the immigrant is slow, awkward, a greenhorn, quickly outpaced by his own children. He is likely to feel inferior, and his children are likely to confirm the feeling. But this sense of inferiority, so painful to him, is also a disaster for them. It cuts them adrift in a world where they are never likely to feel entirely at home. At some point, among themselves, or among their children (the second American generation), a process of recovery begins. Ethnic celebration is a feature of that process. It has a general and a particular form: the celebration of diversity itself and then of the history and culture of a particular group. The first of these, it should be stressed, would be meaningless without the second, for the first is abstract and the second concrete. Pluralism has in itself no powers of survival; it depends upon energy, enthusiasm, commitment within the component groups; it cannot outlast the particularity of cultures and creeds. From the standpoint of the liberal state, particularity is a matter of individual

65

choice, and pluralism nothing more than toleration. From the standpoint of the individual, it is probably something else, for men and women mostly "choose" the culture and creed to which they were born – even if, after conquest or immigration, they have to be born again.

The third function of ethnic assertiveness is to build and sustain the reborn community – to create institutions, gain control of resources, and provide educational and welfare services. As with nation-building, this is hard work, but there is a difficulty peculiar to ethnic groups in a pluralist society: such groups do not have coercive authority over their members. Indeed, they do not have members in the same way that the state has citizens; they have no guaranteed population. Although they are historical communities, they must function as if they were voluntary associations. They must make ethnicity a cause, like prohibition or universal suffrage; they must persuade people to "ethnicize" rather than Americanize themselves. The advocates of religious ethnicity – German Lutherans, Irish Catholics, Jews, and so on – have probably been most successful in doing this. But any group that hopes to survive must commit itself to the same pattern of activity – winning support, raising money, building schools, community centers, and old-age homes.

On the basis of some decades of experience, one can reasonably argue that ethnic pluralism is entirely compatible with the existence of a unified republic. Kallen would have said that it is simply the expression of democracy in the sphere of culture. It is, however, an unexpected expression: the American republic is very different from that described, for example, by Montesquieu and Rousseau. It lacks the intense political fellowship, the commitment to public affairs, that they thought necessary. "The better the constitution of a state is," wrote Rousseau, "the more do public affairs encroach on private in the minds of the citizens. Private affairs are even of much less importance, because the aggregate of the common happiness furnishes a greater proportion of that of each individual, so that there is less for him to seek in particular cares." This is an unlikely description unless ethnic culture and religious belief are closely interwoven with political activity (as Rousseau insisted they should be). It certainly misses the reality of the American republic, where both have been firmly relegated to the private sphere. The emotional life of U.S. citizens is lived mostly in private—which is not to say in solitude, but in groups considerably smaller than the community of all citizens. Americans are communal in their private affairs, individualist in their politics. Civil society is a collection of groups; the state is an organization of individual citizens. And society and state, though they constantly interact, are formally distinct. For support and comfort and a sense of belonging, men and women look to their groups; for freedom and mobility, they look to the state.

Still, democratic participation does bring group members into the political arena where they are likely to discover common interests. Why has this not caused radical divisiveness as in the European empires? It certainly has made for conflict, sometimes of a frightening sort, but always within limits set by the nonterritorial and socially indeterminate character of the immigrant communities and by the sharp divorce of state and ethnicity. No single group can hope to capture the state and turn it into a nation-state. Members of the group are citizens only as Americans, not as Germans, Italians, Irishmen, Jews, or Hispanics. Politics forces them into alliances and coalitions, and democratic politics, because it recognizes each citizen as the equal of every other, without regard to ethnicity,

fosters a unity of individuals alongside the diversity of groups.
American Indians and blacks have mostly been excluded from
this unity, and it is not yet clear on what terms they will be
brought in. But political life is in principle open, and this
openness has served to diffuse the most radical forms of ethnic competition. The result has not been a weak political order: quite the contrary. Though it has not inspired heated
commitment, though politics has not become a mass religion,
the republic has been remarkably stable, and state power has
grown steadily over time.

Towards Corporatism?

The growth of state power sets the stage for a new kind of
pluralist politics. With increasing effect, the state does for all
its citizens what the various groups do or try to do for their
own adherents. It defends their rights, not only against foreign
invasion and domestic violence, but also against persecution, harassment, libel, and discrimination. It celebrates their
collective (American) history, establishing national holidays; building monuments, memorials, and museums; sup-
plying educational materials. It acts to sustain their communal life, collecting taxes and providing a host of welfare
services. The modern state nationalizes communal activity,
and the more energetically it does this, the more taxes it col-
lects, the more services it provides, the harder it becomes for
groups to act on their own. State welfare undercuts private
philanthropy, much of which was organized within ethnic
and religious communities; it makes it harder to sustain
private and parochial schools; it erodes the strength of
cultural institutions.

All this is justified, and more than justified, by the fact that the various groups were radically unequal in strength and in their ability to provide services for their adherents. Moreover, the social coverage of the ethnic communities was uneven and incomplete. Many Americans never looked for services from any particular group, but turned instead to the state. It is not the case that state officials invaded the spheres of welfare and culture; they were invited in by disadvantaged or hardpressed or assimilated citizens. But now, it is said, pluralism cannot survive unless ethnic groups, as well as individuals, share directly in the benefits of state power. Once again, politics must follow ethnicity, recognizing and supporting communal structures.

What does this mean? First, that the state should defend collective as well as individual rights; second, that the state should expand its official celebrations, to include not only its own history but the history of all the peoples that make up the American people; third, that tax money should be fed into the ethnic communities to help in the financing of bilingual and bicultural education and of group-oriented welfare services. And if all this is to be done, and fairly done, then it is necessary also that ethnic groups be given, as a matter of right, some sort of representation within the state agencies that do it.

These are far-reaching claims. They have not received, any more than the earlier pluralism did, a clear theoretical statement. They are the stuff of public pronouncements and political agitation. Their full significance is unclear, but the world they point to is a corporatist world, where ethnic groups no longer organize themselves like voluntary associations but have instead some political standing and legal rights. There is, however, a major difficulty here: groups cannot be assigned rights unless they are first assigned members. There has to be a fixed population with procedures for choosing representa-

69

tives before there can be representatives acting officially on behalf of that population. But ethnic groups in the United States do not have, and never have had, fixed populations (American Indian tribes are a partial exception). Historically, corporatist arrangements have only been worked out for groups that do. In fact, they have only been worked out when the fixity was guaranteed by a rigid dualism, that is, when two communities were locked into a single state: Flemings and Walloons in Belgium, Greeks and Turks in Cyprus, Christians and Muslims in Lebanon. In such cases, people not identified with one community are virtually certain to be identified with the other. The residual category of intermarried couples and aliens will be small, especially if the two communities are anciently established and territorially based. Problems of identification are likely to arise only in the capital city. (Other sorts of problems arise more generally; these examples hardly invite emulation.)

America's immigrant communities have a radically different character. Each of them has a center of active participants, some of them men and women who have been "born-again," and a much larger periphery of individuals and families who are little more than occasional recipients of services generated at the center. They are communities without boundaries, shading off into a residual mass of people who think of themselves simply as Americans. Borders and border guards are among the first products of a successful national liberation movement, but ethnic assertiveness has no similar outcome. There is no way for the various groups to prevent or regulate individual crossings. Nor can the state do this without the most radical coercion of individuals. It cannot fix the population of the groups unless it forces each citizen to choose a single ethnic identity and establishes rigid distinctions among the different identities, of a sort that pluralism by itself has not produced.

It is possible, however, to guarantee representation to ethnic groups without requiring the groups to organize and choose their own spokesmen. The alternative to internal choice is a quota system. Thus, Supreme Court appointments might be constrained by a set of quotas: a certain number of blacks, Jews, Irish and Italian Catholics, and so on, must be serving at any given time. But these men and women would stand in no political relationship to their groups; they would not be responsible agents; nor would they be bound to speak for the interests of their ethnic or religious fellows. They would represent simply by being black (Jewish, Irish) and being *there,* and the Court would be a representative body in the sense that it reflected the pluralism of the larger society in its own membership. It would not matter whether these members came from the center or the periphery of the groups, or whether the groups had clearly defined boundaries, a rich inner life, and so on.

This kind of representation depends only upon external (bureaucratic rather than political) processes, and so it can readily be extended to society at large. Quotas are easy to use in admitting candidates to colleges and professional schools and in hiring them for any sort of employment. Such candidates are not elected but selected, though here, too, there must be a fixed population from which selections can be made. In practice, efforts to identify populations and make quotas possible have been undertaken, with state support, only for oppressed groups. Men and women, marked out as victims or as the children and heirs of victims, have been assigned a right to certain advantages in the selection process; otherwise, it is said, they would not be present at all in schools, professions, and businesses. This is not the place to consider the merits of such a procedure. But it is important to point out that selection by quota functions largely to provide a kind of escape from group life for people whose identity has become a trap. Its chief purpose is to give opportunities to individuals, not a voice to groups. It serves to enhance the wealth and stature of individuals, not necessarily the resources of the ethnic community. The community is strengthened, to be sure, if newly trained men and women return to work among its members, but only a small minority do that. Mostly, they serve, if they serve at all, as role models for other upwardly mobile men and women. When weak and hitherto passive groups mobilize themselves in order to win a place in the quota system, they do so for the sake of that mobility, and are likely to have no further raison d'etre once it is achieved.

Considered more generally, there is a certain tension between quota systems and ethnic pluralism, for the administrators of any such system are bound to refuse to recognize differences among the groups. They come by their numbers through simple mathematical calculations. It would be intolerable for them to make judgments as to the character or quality of the different cultures. The tendency of their work, then, is to reproduce within every group to which quotas are applied the same educational and employment patterns. Justice is a function of the identity of the patterns among groups rather than of life chances among individuals. But it is clear that ethnic pluralism by itself would not generate any such identity. Historically specific cultures necessarily produce historically specific patterns of interest and work. This is not to say that pluralism necessarily militates against egalitarian principles, since equality might well take the form (socialists have always expected it to take the form) of roughly equal recompense for different kinds of work. It is not implausible to imagine a heterogeneous but egalitarian society: the heterogeneity, cultural and private; the equality, economic and political. Quotas point, by contrast, toward group uniformity, not individual equality. Though it would be necessary for individuals to identify themselves (or to be identified) as group members in order to receive the benefits of a quota system, these identifications would progressively lose their communal significance. The homogenization of the groups would open the way for the assimilation of their members into a prevailing or evolving national culture.

State and Ethnicity

The state can intervene in two basic ways to structure group life. It can encourage or require the groups to organize themselves in corporatist fashion, assigning a political role to the corporations in the state apparatus. This is the autonomist strategy, the nearest thing to national liberation that is possible under conditions of multiethnicity. The effect of autonomy would be to intensify and institutionalize cultural difference. Alternatively, the state can act to reduce differences among groups by establishing uniform or symmetrical achievement standards for their members. Each group would be represented, though not through any form of collective action, in roughly equal proportions in every area of political, social, and economic life. This is the integrationist strategy. It can be applied in a limited and compensatory way to particular (oppressed) groups or more generally to all groups. Applied generally, its effect would be to repress every sort of cultural specificity, turning ethnic identity into an administrative classification.

What the state cannot do is to reproduce politically the pluralist pattern that the immigrants and their children have spontaneously generated, for that pattern is inherently fluid and indeterminate. Its existence depends upon keeping apart what nation-state and corporatist theory bring together: a state organized coercively to protect rights, a society organized on voluntarist principles to advance interests (including cultural and religious interests). State officials provide a framework within which groups can flourish but cannot guarantee their flourishing or even their survival. The only way to provide such guarantees would be to introduce coercion into the social world, transforming the groups into something like their Old World originals and denying the whole experience of immigration, individualism, and communal rebirth. Nothing like this would appear to be on the American agenda.

The survival and flourishing of the groups depends largely upon the vitality of their centers. If that vitality cannot be sustained, pluralism will prove to be a temporary phenomenon, a way-station on the road to American nationalism. The early pluralists may have been naive in their calm assurance that ethnic vitality would have an enduring life. But they were surely right to insist that it should not artificially be kept alive, any more than it should be repressed, by state power. On the other hand, there is an argument to be made, against the early pluralists, in favor of providing some sorts of public support for ethnic activity. It is an argument familiar from economic analysis, having to do with the character of ethnicity as a collective good.

Individual mobility is the special value but also the characteristic weakness of American pluralism. It makes for loose relations between center and periphery; it generates a world without boundaries. In that world, the vitality of the center is tested by its ability to hold on to peripheral men and women and to shape their self-images and their convictions. These men and women, in turn, live off the strength of the center, which they do not have to pay for either in time or money. They are religious and cultural freeloaders, their lives enhanced by a community they do not actively support and by an identity they need not themselves cultivate. There is no way to charge them for what they receive from the center, except when they receive specific sorts of material help. But their most important gain may be nothing more than a certain sense of pride, an aura of ethnicity, otherwise unavailable. Nor is there anything unjust in their freeloading. The people at the center are not being exploited; they want to hold the periphery. Freeloading of this sort is probably inevitable in a free society.

But so long as it exists – that is, so long as ethnicity is experienced as a collective good by large numbers of people – it probably makes sense to permit collective money, taxpayers' money, to seep through the state/ethnic group (state/church) barrier. This is especially important when taxes constitute a significant portion of the national wealth and when the state has undertaken, on behalf of all its citizens, to organize education and welfare. It can be done in a variety of ways, through tax exemptions and rebates, subsidies, matching grants, certificate plans, and so on. The precise mechanisms do not matter, once it is understood that they must stop short of a corporatist system, requiring no particular form of ethnic organization and no administrative classification of members. A rough fairness in the distribution of funds is probably ensured by the normal workings of democratic politics in a

heterogenous society. Ticket-balancing and coalition-build-
ing will provide ethnic groups with a kind of informal representation in the allocative process. Democratic politics can be
remarkably accommodating to groups, so long as it has to deal
only with individuals: voters, candidates, welfare recipients,
taxpayers, criminals, all without official ethnic tags. And the
accommodation need not be bitterly divisive, though it is sure
to generate conflict. Ethnic citizens can be remarkably loyal to
a state that protects and fosters private communal life, if that
is seen to be equitably done.

The question still remains whether this kind of equity,
adapted to the needs of immigrant communities, can successfully be extended to the racial minorities now asserting their
own group claims. Racism is the great barrier to a fully developed pluralism and as long as it exists American Indians and
blacks, and perhaps Mexican-Americans as well, will be
tempted by (and torn between) the anti-pluralist alternatives
of corporate division and state-sponsored unification. It would
be presumptuous to insist that these options are foolish or
unwarranted so long as opportunities for group organization
and cultural expression are not equally available to all Americans. A state committed to pluralism, however, cannot do anything more than see to it that those opportunities are *available,*
not that they are used, and it can only do that by ensuring that
all citizens, without reference to their groups, share equally, or
roughly equally, in the resources of American life.

Beyond that, distributive justice among groups is bound
to be relative to the vitality of their centers and of their committed members. Short of corporatism, the state cannot help
groups unable or unwilling to help themselves. It cannot save
them from ultimate Americanization. Indeed, it works so as to
permit individual escape (assimilation and intermarriage) as

well as collective commitment. The primary function of the state, and of politics generally, is to do justice to individuals, and in a pluralist society ethnicity is simply one of the background conditions of this effort. Ethnic identification gives meaning to the lives of many men and women, but it has nothing to do with their standing as citizens. This distinction seems worth defending even if it makes for a world in which there are no guarantees of meaning. In a culturally homogeneous society the government can foster a particular identity, deliberately merging culture and politics. This the U.S. government cannot do. Pluralism is thus still an experiment, still to be tested against the long-term historical and theoretical power of the nation-state.

CIVILITY AND CIVIC VIRTUE
IN CONTEMPORARY AMERICA

Decline and fall is the most common historical perception, even among intellectuals. I want to examine this perception in its most important contemporary form, which is also a recurrent form. "We have physicists, geometers, chemists, astronomers, poets, musicians, painters," wrote Rousseau in 1750, "we no longer have citizens. . . ."[1] Here in the United States we still do have citizens, but it is frequently said of them that their commitment to the political community is less profound than it once was, that there has been a decline of civic virtue and even of ordinary civility, an erosion of the moral and political qualities that make a good citizen. It is hard to know how to judge statements of this kind. They suggest comparisons without specifying any historical reference point. They seem to be prompted by a variety of tendencies and events which are by no means uniform in character or necessarily connected: the extent of draft resistance during the Vietnam War, the domestic violence of the middle and late 1960s, the recent challenges to academic freedom, the new acceptance of pornography, the decline in the fervor with which national holidays are celebrated, and so on.

1 Jean-Jacques Rousseau, "Discourse on the Sciences and Arts," in *The First and Second Discourses*, edited by Roger D. Masters (New York: St. Martin's Press, 1964), p. 59.

Perhaps one way of judging these (and other) phenomena is to ask what it is we expect of citizens – of citizens in general but also of American citizens in particular, members of a liberal democracy, each of whom represents, as Rousseau would have said, only 1/200,000,000th of the general will. What do we expect of one another? I am going to suggest a list of common expectations; I shall try to make it an exhaustive list. Working our way through it, we shall see that we are the citizens we ought to be, given the social and political order in which we live. And if critics of our citizenship remain dissatisfied, then it will be time to ask how that order might be changed.

Loyalty, Service, Civility

1. We expect some degree of commitment or loyalty – but to what? Not to *la patrie,* the fatherland; that concept has never captured the American imagination, probably because so many of us were fathered in other lands. Not to the nation; the appearance of an American nationality was for a long time the goal of our various immigrant absorption systems, but this goal has stood in some tension with the practical (and now with the ideological) pluralism of our society. Most of those who mourn our lost civility would not, I think, be happy with an American nationalism. Not to the state, conceived abstractly, but only to a particular kind of state: our allegiance is to the republic. Now that is a very special kind of commitment, stripped of the mystical connotations of loyalty in Old World countries. We stand, partly by necessity, partly by choice, on narrower ground. Ours is a political allegiance, and our politics is Judaic or puritan in character; it does not lend itself to ritu-

alistic elaboration. Our holidays are occasions for speeches, not for ceremonial communions; our inaugurations are without sacramental significance. We are rightly unwilling to make spectacles of our celebrations, and for that reason it has been virtually impossible to adapt them to the needs of a mass society. There is a certain cynicism today about the symbolic expressions of American loyalty – perhaps because no one can imagine 200,000,000 people celebrating the Fourth of July, simultaneously and together, in some way that isn't repellent to liberal sensibilities. Surely it is a commendable feature of our public life that we do not press the occasion upon our citizens.

Our passivity in this regard probably has something to do with the triumph of secularism in the republic. The content of many American celebrations – Memorial Day and Thanksgiving, for example – is or was markedly religious in character and must lose much of its resonance as religion loses its hold. On the other hand, we have always denied that any particular religious belief or even religious belief in general was necessary in an American citizen. Now that denial is being tested, not as to its justice, but as to its practicality. Understandably, people are worried; for it is often said that loyalty has to be collectively symbolized and acted out if it is to be sustained. The appropriate symbols and actions, however, must grow naturally out of our common life; they cannot be invented, conjured up, pulled out of a politician's hat. If we have not tried to substitute the goddess Reason for the Christian God, as Robespierre tried to do in France, surely that too is to our credit. But the symbols and actions don't grow naturally, and liberal loyalty seems to be sustained in some other way – not through communal celebrations but through private enjoyments, as writers like John Locke undoubtedly intended. One gets a different kind, and perhaps a different degree, of loyalty then, but there is no reason to think that one doesn't get the kind and degree a liberal republic requires.

2. We expect citizens to defend their country, even to risk their lives in its defense. In American lore, the minuteman, who rushes to arms when his country is in danger, long ago came to represent the citizen at his best. But it has to be said that this colonial hero and his successors, the militiamen of the nineteenth century, were essentially volunteers who did not always agree with the politicians in the capital or even with their local commanders as to when the country was in danger. They claimed a kind of local option which was for years the despair of American military planners.[2] Nor is it, after all, any sign of civic virtue merely to rush to arms. In August 1914, Austrians and Germans, Frenchmen and Englishmen, flooded the enlistment offices, but we would not want to explain their military enthusiasm by reference to the quality of their citizenship. Indeed, in an earlier America, the readiness of the inhabitants of the Old World to die at the behest of their states and sovereigns would more likely have been understood as a sign of the poverty of their lives and their lack of moral independence. The same attitude explains the old American hatred of conscription. It was thought an infringement of individual liberty and a sure sign of tyrannical government when family and home were invaded and young men dragged off to war. When James Monroe, then Secretary of War, first proposed a draft in 1814, Daniel Webster assured him that the country would not stand for it:

> In my opinion, Sir, the sentiments of the free population of this country are greatly mistaken here. The nation is not yet in a temper to submit to conscription. The people have too fresh and strong a feeling of

2 See Marcus Cunliffe, *Soldiers and Civilians: The Martial Spirit in America, 1775-1865* (Boston: Little, Brown, 1968), especially chaps. 6 and 7.

the blessings of civil liberty to be willing thus to surrender to it. . .
Laws, Sir, of this nature can create nothing but opposition. A military
force cannot be raised, in this manner, but by the means of a military
force. If the administration has found that it cannot form an army
without conscription, it will find, if it ventures on these experiments,
that it cannot enforce conscription without an army.[3]

We have come a long way since those days, a way marked as
much by changes in the external world as in our domestic society. The domestic changes have been made only gradually and,
as Webster predicted, in the face of constant opposition. It is
worth remembering how recent a creation the docile draftee is
before we mourn his disappearance (has he disappeared?) as a
loss of American virtue. In 1863, the first conscription law was
fiercely resisted – over one thousand people died in the New
York draft riot of that year – and it was massively evaded during the remainder of the Civil War. The draft was still being
evaded on a large scale in World War I, particularly in rural
areas where it was easy to hide. And who can say that the
young men who took to the woods in 1917 were not reaffirm-
ing the values of an earlier America? They would have grabbed
their rifles readily enough had the Boche marched into Ken-
tucky. Perhaps that is the only true test of their citizenship.

The citizen-soldier defends his hearth and home, and he
also defends the political community within which the enjoy-
ment of hearth and home is made possible. His fervor is
heightened when that community is in danger. Armies of citizens, like those of Rome or the first French Republic or Israel
today, are born in moments of extreme peril. Once the peril
abates, the fervor declines. The armies of great powers must be
sustained on a different basis, and the long-term considerations that lead them to fight here or there, in other people's

3 Speech in the House of Representatives, December 9, 1814, reprinted in Lillian Schlis-
sel, ed., *Conscience in America* (New York: E. P. Dutton, 1968), pp. 70-71.

countries, when there is no immediate or visible threat to their own, can hardly be expected to evoke among their citizens a passionate sense of duty. Perhaps these citizens have an obligation to fight, in obedience, say, to laws democratically enacted, but this is not the same obligation that American publicists meant to stress when they made the minuteman a mythic figure. It has more to do with law-abidance than with civic courage or dedication.

3. We expect citizens to obey the law and to maintain a certain decorum of behavior – a decorum that is commonly called civility. That word once had to do more directly with the political virtues of citizenship: one of its obsolescent meanings is "civil righteousness." But it has come increasingly to denote only social virtues; orderliness, politeness, seemliness are the synonyms the dictionary suggests, and these terms, though it is no doubt desirable that they describe our public life, orient us quite decisively toward the private realm. Perhaps this shift in meaning is a sign of our declining dedication to republican values, but it actually occurred some time ago and does not reflect on ourselves and our contemporaries. For some time, we have thought that *good behavior* is what we could rightly expect from a citizen, and the crucial form of good behavior is everyday law-abidance. Has this expectation been disappointed? Certainly many people write as if it has been. I am inclined to think them wrong, though not for reasons that have much to do with republican citizenship.

If we could measure the rate and intensity of obedience to law – not merely the nonviolation of the penal code, but the interest, the concern, the anxiety with which citizens *aim* at obedience – I am certain we would chart a fairly steady upward movement in every modernizing country, at least after the initial crisis of modernization is past. Contemporary societies require and sustain a very intense form of social discipline, and this discipline is probably more pervasive and more successfully internalized than was that of peasant societies or of small towns and villages. We have only to think about our own lives to realize the extent of our submission to what Max Weber called "rational-legal authority." It is reflected in our time sense, our ability to work hard and methodically, our acceptance of bureaucratic hierarchies, our habitual orientation to rules and regulations. Consider, for example, the simple but surprising fact that each of us will, before April 15, carefully fill out a government form detailing our incomes and calculating the tax we owe the United States – which we will then promptly pay. The medieval tithe, if it was ever a realistic tax, was socially enforced; our own tax is individually enforced. We ourselves are the calculators and the collectors; the tax system could not succeed without our conscientiousness. Surely the American income tax is a triumph of civilization. There are very few political orders within which one can imagine such a system working; I doubt that it would have worked, for example, in Tocqueville's America.

But I want to turn to two other examples of our relative civility which speak more directly to the concerns of our recent past, which have to do, that is, with violence. In 1901, David Brewer, an associate justice of the U.S. Supreme Court, delivered a series of lectures on American citizenship at Yale University, in the course of which he worried at some length about the prevalence of vigilante justice and lynch law.[4] This was the peculiarly American way of "not tarrying for the magistrate." "It may almost be regarded," Brewer said, "as a habit

---

4 David Brewer, *American Citizenship* (New York: C. Scribner's Sons, 1902), pp. 102 ff. From the same period, see also James E. Cutler, *Lynch-Law: An Investigation into the History of Lynching in the United States* (New York: Longmans, Green, 1905).

of the American people." Clearly, our habits have changed; in this respect, at least, we have grown more law-abiding since the turn of the century. The police sometimes take the law into their own hands, but they are our only vigilantes; ordinary citizens rarely act in the old American way. This is not the result of a more highly developed civic consciousness, but it is a matter of improved social discipline, and it also suggests that, despite our popular culture, we are less ready for violence, less accustomed to violence, than were earlier generations of American citizens.

We are also less given to riot; if nineteenth-century statistics are at all reliable, our mobs are less dangerous to human life. The most striking thing about the urban riots of the 1960s, apart from the surprise that greeted them, for which our history offers no justification, is the relatively small number of people who were actually killed in their course. By all accounts, riots were once much bloodier: I have already mentioned New York's "bloody week" of 1863. They also seem to have been more exuberantly tumultuous, and the tumult more accepted in the life of the time. Here, for example, are a set of newspaper headlines from New York in 1834:[5]

> A Bloody Fight
> Mayor and Officers Wounded
> Mob Triumphant
> The Streets Blocked by Fifteen Thousand Enraged Whigs
> Military Called Out

These lines describe an election riot, not uncommon in an age when party loyalties were considerably more intense than they are now and a far higher proportion of the eligible voters were likely to turn out on election day. The accompanying news story does not suggest that the rioters or their leaders were extremists or revolutionaries. They apparently were ordinary citizens.

5 Quoted in Cunliffe, *Soldiers and Civilians*, p. 93.

Our own riots are also the work of ordinary citizens, but not of the contemporary equivalents of Whigs, Orangemen, or even Know-Nothings. Riots today seem to be peculiarly disorganized, each of them less a communal event than a series of simultaneous acts of individual desperation. They are more frightening than the earlier riots and also less dangerous. Perhaps this change is appropriate to a liberal society: if civility is privatized, then so must incivility be. Crime in contemporary America is something like a diffused, disintegrated riot.

This last example suggests a certain tension between civility and republican citizenship. Indeed, in the early modern period, one of the chief arguments against republicanism was that it made for disorder and tumult. Faction fights, party intrigue, street wars; instability and sedition: these were the natural forms of political life in what Thomas Hobbes called "the Greek and Roman anarchies," and so it would be, he argued, in any similar regime.[6] He may have been right, in some limited sense at least. The improvement in social discipline seems to have been accompanied by a decline in political passion, in that lively sense of public involvement that presumably characterized the enraged Whigs of 1834 and other early Americans. I shall have more to say about this when I turn to the general issue of political participation. But first it is necessary to take up another aspect of our new civility.

Tolerance, Participation

4. We expect citizens to be tolerant of one another. This is probably as close as we can come to that "friendship" which Aristotle thought should characterize relations among mem-

6 *De Cive*, XII 3

bers of the same political community. For friendship is only possible within a relatively small and homogeneous city, but toleration reaches out infinitely. Once certain barriers of feeling and belief have been broken down, it is as easy to tolerate five million people as to tolerate five. Hence toleration is a crucial form of civility in all modern societies and especially in our own. But it is not easily achieved. Much of the violence of American history has been the work of men and women resisting its advance in the name of one or another form of local and particularized friendship or in the name of those systems of hierarchy and segregation that served in the past to make pluralism possible. It's probably fair to say that resistance has grown weaker in recent years; the United States is a more tolerant society today than at any earlier period of its history. Of course, we need to be more tolerant; it's as if, once we commit ourselves to toleration, the demand for it escalates; it is no longer a question of a recognized range of religious and political dissidence, but of the margins beyond the range. Even the margins are safer today; more people live there and with less fear of public harassment and social pressure. It is precisely these people, however, who seem to pose a problem for us, who lead us to worry about the future of civic virtue. A curious and revealing fact, for their very existence is a sign of our civility.

The problem is that many Americans who find it easy (more or less) to tolerate racial and religious and even political differences find it very hard to tolerate sexual deviance and countercultural lifestyles. One day, perhaps, this difficulty will be remembered only as a passing moment in the painful development of an open society. But it doesn't feel that way now; it feels much more drastic, so that intelligent people talk of the end of civilization, all coherence gone, the fulfillment of this or that modernist nightmare. For surely (they say) political society requires and rests upon *some* shared values, a certain spiritual cohesion, however limited in character. And a commitment to moral laissez-faire does not provide any cohesion at all. It undermines the very basis of a common life, because the ethic of toleration leads us to make our peace with every refusal of commonality. So we drift apart, losing through our very acceptance of one another's differences all sense of kinship and solidarity.

This is undoubtedly overstated, for the fact is that we do coexist, not only Protestants, Catholics, and Jews; blacks and whites; but also Seventh Day Adventists, Buddhists, and Black Muslims; Birchers and Trotskyites; sexual sectarians of every sort, homo and hetero. Nor is it a small thing that we have made our peace with all these, for the only alternative, if history has any lessons at all, is cruelty and repression. Liberalism may widen our differences as it widens the range of permissible difference, but it also generates a pattern of accommodation that we ought to value. It would be foolish to value it, however, without noticing that, like other forms of civility, this pattern of accommodation is antithetical to political activism. It tends to insulate politics from group conflict, to promote among citizens a general indifference toward the opinions of their fellows, to freeze the intolerant out of public life (they are disproportionately represented, for example, among nonvoters). It stands in the way of the personal transformations and new commitments that might grow out of a more open pattern of strife and contention. It makes for political peace; it makes politics less dangerous and less interesting. And yet our notions about citizenship lead us to demand precisely that citizens *be interested* in politics.

5. We expect citizens to participate actively in political life. Republicanism is a form of collective self-government, and its success requires, at the very least, that large numbers of citizens vote and that smaller numbers join in parties and movements, in meetings and demonstrations. No doubt, such acivity is in part self-regarding, but any stable commitment probably has to be based and is in fact usually based on some notion of the public good. It is, then, virtuous activity; interest in public issues and devotion to public causes are the key signs of civic virtue.

Voting is the minimal form of virtuous conduct, but it is also the easiest to measure, and if we take it as a useful index, we can be quite precise in talking about the character of our citizenship. Participation in elections, as Walter Dean Burnham has shown, was very high in the nineteenth century, not only in presidential contests, but also in off-year congressional and even in local elections.[7] Something like four-fifths of the eligible voters commonly went to the polls. "The nineteenth century American political system," writes Burnham, ". . .was incomparably the most thoroughly democratized of any in the world." A sharp decline began around 1896 and continued through the 1920s, when the number of eligible voters actually voting fell to around two-fifths. Rates of participation rose in the 1930s, leveled off, rose again in the 1950s, leveled off again – without coming close to the earlier figures. Today, the percentage of American citizens who are consistent nonparticipants is about twice what it was in the 1890s. By this measure, then, we are less virtuous than were nineteenth-century Americans, less committed to the public business.

7 Walter Dean Burnham, "The Changing Shape of the American Political Universe," *The American Political Science Review*, LIX (March 1965), 7-28.

The reasons for this decline are not easy to sort out. Burnham suggests that it may have something to do with the final consolidation of power by the new industrial elites. The triumph of corporate bureaucracy was hardly conducive to a participatory politics among members of the new working class or among those farmers who had been the backbone of the Populist movement. Some workers turned to socialism (Debs got a million votes in 1912), but far more dropped out of the political system altogether. They became habitual nonvoters, at least until the CIO brought many of the men and women it organized back into electoral politics in the 1930s. If this account is right—and other accounts are possible—then nonvoting can be seen as a rational response to certain sorts of social change. No doubt it was also functional to the social system as a whole. The decline in participation during a period of increasing heterogeneity and rapid urbanization probably helped stabilize the emerging patterns of law-abidance and toleration. Certainly American society would have been far more turbulent than it was had new immigrants, urban dwellers, and industrial workers been actively involved in politics. That is not to argue that they shouldn't have been involved, only that people who set a high value on civility shouldn't complain about their lack of civic virtue.

A recent study of political acts more "difficult" than voting—giving money, attending meetings, joining organizations—suggests that there was a considerable increase in participation in the course of the 1960s.[8] Not surprisingly, this increase coincided with a period of turmoil and dissension of which it was probably both cause and effect. One might impartially have watched the events of that time and worried about the

8 Sidney Verba and Norman H. Nie, *Participation in America: Political Democracy and Social Equality* (New York: Harper & Row, 1972), especially chap. 14.

loss of civility and rejoiced in the resurgence of civic virtue. The connection between the two is clear enough: people are mobilized for political action, led to commit themselves and to make the sacrifices and take the risks commitment requires, only when significant public issues are seized upon by the agitators and organizers of movements and parties and made the occasion for exciting confrontations. These need not be violent confrontations; violence draws spectators more readily than participants. But if the issues are significant, if the conflict is serious, violence always remains a possibility. The only way to avoid the possibility is to avoid significant issues or to make it clear that the democratic political struggle is a charade whose outcome won't affect the resolution of the issues – and then rates of participation will quickly drop off.

The civil rights and antiwar agitations of the 1960s demonstrate that there are still dedicated citizens in the United States. But the activity generated by those movements turned out to be evanescent, leaving behind no organizational residue, no basis for an ongoing participatory politics. Perhaps that is because not enough people committed themselves. The national mood, if one focuses on the silence of the silent majority, is tolerant and passive – in much the same way as it was tolerant and passive in the face of prohibitionists or suffragettes or even socialists and communists in the 1930s: that is, there is no demand for massive repression and there is no major upsurge in political involvement. It is also important, I think, that the two movements of the sixties did not link up in any stable way with either of the established parties. Instead of strengthening party loyalty, they may well have contributed to a further erosion. If that is so, even rates of electoral participation will probably fall in the coming years, for parties are the crucial media of political activism. These two failures – to mobilize mass support, to connect with the established parties – may well suggest the general pattern of political life in America today. For most of our citizens, politics is no vocation. They think it a duty to vote, but they have no deep commitment to a creed or party, and only about half of them bother to vote. Beyond that, they are wrapped up in their private affairs and committed to the orderliness and proprieties of the private realm. Though they are tolerant, up to a point, of political activists, they regard politics as an intrusion and they easily resist the temptations of the arena. This makes life hard for the smaller number of citizens who are intermittently moved by some public issue and who seek to move their fellows. It may help explain the frenetic quality of their zeal and the way some of them drift, in extreme cases, into depression and madness. The institutional structures and the mass commitment necessary to sustain civic virtue simply don't exist in contemporary America.

Participatory Politics

The ideals of citizenship do not today make a coherent whole. The citizen receives, so to speak, inconsistent instruction. Patriotism, civility, toleration, and political activism pull him in different directions. The first and last require a kind of zeal – that is, they require both passion and conviction – and they make for excitement and tumult in public life. It is often said that the worst wars are civil wars because they are fought between brethren. One might say something similar about republican politics: because it rests on a shared commitment, it is often more bitter and divisive than politics in other regimes. Civility and tolerance serve to reduce the tension, but they do so by undercutting the commitment. They encourage people to view their interests as fragmented, diverse, and private; they make for quiet and passive citizens, unwilling to intrude on others or to subject themselves to the discipline of a creed or party. I am not going to argue that we need choose in some absolute way one or the other of these forms of political life. What exists today and what will always exist is some balance between them. But the balance has changed over the years: we are, I think, more civil and less civically virtuous than Americans once were. The new balance is a liberal one, and there can be little doubt that it fits the scale and complexity of modern society and the forms of economic organization developed in the United States in the twentieth century. What has occurred is not a decline and fall but a working out of liberal values – individualism, secularism, toleration – and at the same time an adjustment to the demands of capitalist modernity.

The new citizenship, however, leaves many Americans dissatisfied. Liberalism, even at its most permissive, is a hard politics because it offers so few emotional rewards; the liberal state is not a home for its citizens; it lacks warmth and intimacy. And so contemporary dissatisfaction takes the form of a yearning for political community, passionate affirmation, explicit patriotism. These are dangerous desires, for they cannot readily be met within the world of liberalism. They leave us open to a politics I would find unattractive and even frightening: a willful effort to build social cohesion and political enthusiasm from above, as it were, through the use of state power. Imagine a charismatic leader, talking about American values and goals, making war on pornography and sexual deviance (and then on political and social deviance), establishing loyalty oaths and new celebrations, rallying the people for some real or imagined crisis. The prospect is hard to imagine without the crisis, but given that, might it not be genuinely appealing to men and women cut off from a common life, feeling little connection with their neighbors and little connection with the past or future of the republic? It would offer solidarity in a time of danger, and the hard truth about individualism, secularism, and toleration is that they make solidarity very difficult. The recognition of this truth helps explain, I think, the gradual drift of some American intellectuals toward a kind of communal conservatism. Thus, the fulsome debate, some years ago, about our "national purpose" (a liberal nation can have no collective purpose) and the new interest in the possibilities of censorship, both of which suggest the desire to shape citizens in a common mold and to raise the pitch of their virtue.

Even assuming these are the right goals, however, that is the wrong way to reach them. It begins on the wrong side of the balance, with an attack on the heterogeneity of liberal society, and so it poses a threat to all our (different) beliefs, values, and ways of life. I want to suggest that we start on the other side, by expanding the possibilities for a participatory politics. In the liberal world, patriotic feeling and political participation depend on one another, it seems to me, in a special way. For Rousseau and for classical republicans generally, these two rested and could only rest on social, religious, and cultural unity. They were the political expressions of a homogeneous people. One might say that, for them, citizenship was only possible where it was least necessary, where politics was nothing more than the extension into the public arena of a common life that began and was sustained outside. Under such conditions, as John Stuart Mill wrote of the ancient republics and the Swiss cities, patriotism is easy; it is a "passion of spontaneous growth."[9] But today, society, religion, and culture are pluralist in form; there is no common life outside the arena, and there is less and less spontaneous patriotism. The only thing that we can share is the republic itself, the business of government. Only if we actually do share that are we *fellow* citizens. Without that, we are private men and women, radically disjoined, confined to a sphere of existence which, however rich it can be and is in liberal society, can never satisfy our longing for political excitement, for meaningful citizenship, for public causes and effects.

Among people like ourselves, a community of patriots would have to be sustained by politics alone. I don't know if such a community is possible. Judged by the theory and practice of the classical republics, its creation certainly seems unlikely: how can a common citizenship develop if there is no other commonality – no ethnic solidarity, no established religion, no unified cultural tradition? When I argued that the contemporary balance of civility and civic virtue is appropriate to a liberal society, I was making the classic case for a causal connection between society and state, everyday life and political commitment. I did not mean, however, to make a determinist case. One can always strain at the limits of the appropriate; one can always act inappropriately. And it is not implausible to suggest that social circumstance, like Machiavelli's fortune, is the arbiter of only half of what we do. Given liberal society and culture, certain sorts of dedication may well lie beyond our reach. But that's not to say that we cannot, so to speak, enlarge the time and space within which we live as citizens. This is the working principle of democratic social-

9 John Stuart Mill, "M. de Tocqueville on Democracy in America," in *The Philosophy of John Stuart Mill,* edited by Marshall Cohen (New York: Modern Library, 1961), p. 158.

ism: that politics can be opened up, rates of participation significantly increased, decision-making really shared, without a full-scale attack on private life and liberal values, without a religious revival or a cultural revolution. What is necessary is the expansion of the public sphere. I don't mean by that the growth of state power—which will come anyway, for a stronger state is the necessary and natural antidote to liberal disintegration—but a new politicizing of the state, a devolution of state power into the hands of ordinary citizens.

Three kinds of expansion are required. They add up to a familiar program which I can only sketch in the briefest possible way: a radical democratization of corporate government, so that crucial decisions about the shape of the economy are clearly seen to be the public's business; the decentralization of governmental activity so as to alter the scale of political life and increase the numbers of men and women able to play an effective part in everyday decision-making; the creation of parties and movements that can operate at different levels of government and claim a greater degree of individual commitment at every level than our present parties can. All this is needed if patriotism is to be nourished, in the absence of social and cultural cohesion, by what Mill calls "artificial means," that is, "a large and frequent intervention of the citizens in the management of public business."[10]

How such an intervention might actually be achieved, I cannot consider here. It is more important for my present purposes to acknowledge that achieving it (or trying to) will significantly raise the levels of intensity and contention in our

10 Mill, *The Philosophy of John Stuart Mill*, p. 159. I should stress that I believe these "artificial means" to include economic as well as political self-management. I don't think this is an unfair extension of Mill's meaning. A natural patriotism for him was one generated by all those social qualities that we possess, so to speak, without having to make them for ourselves; an artificial patriotism derives from conscious activity.

politics, and even the levels of intolerance and zeal. Militancy, righteousness, indignation, and hostility are the very stuff of politics. The interventions of the people are not like those of the Holy Ghost. For the people bring with them into the arena all the contradictions of liberal society and culture. And the political arena is in any case a setting for confrontation. Politics (unlike economics) is inherently competitive, and when the competition takes place among large groups of citizens rather than among the king's favorites or rival cliques of oligarchs, it is bound to be more expressive, more feverish, and more tumultuous.

And yet it is only in the arena that we can hope for a solidarity that is spontaneous and free. *E pluribus unum* is an alchemist's promise; out of liberal pluralism no oneness can come. But there is a kind of sharing that is possible even with conflict and perhaps only with it. In the arena, rival politicians have to speak about the common good, even if they simultaneously advance sectional interests. Citizens learn to ask, in addition to their private questions, what the common good really is. In the course of sustained political activity enemies become familiar antagonists, known to be asking the same (contradictory) questions. Men and women who merely tolerated one another's differences recognize that they share a commitment – to *this* arena and to the people in it. Even a divisive election, then, is a ritual of unity, not only because it has a single outcome, but also because it reaffirms the existence of the arena itself, the public thing, and the sovereign people. Politics is a school of loyalty, through which we make the republic our moral possession and come to regard it with a kind of reverence. And election day is the republic's most important celebration. I don't want to exaggerate the awe a citizen feels when he votes, but I do think there is awe, and a sense of pride, at least when the issues being decided are really important and the political order is built to a human scale. There can even be civility in the arena, courtesy, generosity, a concern for rules (especially, as in war, among professionals and veterans) – though one must expect something else much of the time.

In saying all this, I am repeating an argument that Lewis Coser made in the 1950s in his book *The Functions of Social Conflict.* The argument is worth repeating since the conflicts of subsequent decades do not seem to have confirmed it for most Americans. Nor would it be irrational to recognize, with Coser, the "integrative functions of antagonistic behavior" and decide, nonetheless, to live with some lesser degree of integration.[11] I am inclined to think that we can have civility and law-abidance without any intensification of patriotism and participation. No doubt, the present balance is unstable, but so is every other; we have to choose the difficulties we shall live with. What we cannot have, and ought not to ask of one another, under present conditions, is civic virtue. For that we must first create a new politics. I have tried to suggest that it must be a socialist and democratic politics and that it must not supersede but stand in constant tension with the liberalism of our society.

11 Lewis A. Coser, *The Functions of Social Conflict* (Glencoe, Ill.: Free Press, 1956), chap. 7.

CONSTITUTIONAL RIGHTS
AND THE SHAPE OF CIVIL SOCIETY

The Two Texts

The Constitution of the United States is really two separate documents, two texts, written at different times, for different purposes, at the behest of different people. The first text is the original unamended seven articles, the Constitution itself; the second text is the Bill of Rights, the first ten amendments plus those parts of the original articles and of subsequent amendments that are now read in terms of rights theory. The two are dissimilar in style, opposite to one another as political programs, and intimately joined in practice.

The first text provides a design for state and government. Its purpose is to create a strong and centralized regime restrained by a set of internal, institutional checks and balances. The political machinery is meant to be powerful; the restraints are built in, part of the machine and not dependent on the good will or political intelligence of the operators of the machine. The Founders did not have much faith in anyone's good will, though they were, it has to be said, fairly confident at least about their own political intelligence. That confidence doesn't seem today to have been mistaken. The machinery they designed has no doubt been used in ways they did not foresee and would not have approved, but it is, two hundred years later, almost entirely in place. Current proposals for changing it (the six-year presidential term, for example) are of the tinkering sort, a tribute to the enduring value of what is being tinkered with. That is not to say, obviously, that the Constitution makes it impossible for political leaders to behave stupidly or immorally. But it does make it unlikely that a leader behaving in such a way won't encounter institutional opposition. Somewhere in the state machine, officials will find it in their personal interest, or in the interest of their offices, to scrutinize, criticize, resist, and counteract the policies of the leader. He will then complain that something is wrong with the machine; he can't make it run. But that's what the machine is like; that's when it is running according to its constitutional design.

If the first text is focused on the state, the second text is focused on civil society. It is in part the work of men who were worried by the state machine and who were critical of the specific design of the Founders. The second text opposes the first: its most passionate advocates had little confidence in the internal checks and balances; they insisted instead on a set of external restraints, a statement of principles, a "bill" of rights.[1] The Bill is meant to fix the boundaries of future state action: all that is most valued in civil society lies on the other side, off limits. Churches, political assemblies, newspapers, private homes, and finally individual men and women are protected against political interventions. (The separate states are also protected, but I shall not focus on them just now.)

1 See *The Anti-Federalists,* ed. Cecelia M. Kenyon (Indianapolis: Bobbs-Merrill, 1966), pp. xxxviii, lxx, 186-89, 193-233.

By and large the external restraints have held or, at least, they have been restored after each partial collapse; they have never collapsed entirely. This is so only because they were incorporated into the machine itself, admitted to a central role in the regime of checks and balances. The Supreme Court has made the Bill of Rights its own bill of entitlement and has undertaken actively to enforce what would otherwise be a merely hortatory document. It is not the case that the Court's claim to "judicial review" hangs on the Bill; it was first asserted on the basis of what appears to be an unproblematic account of judicial jurisdiction, part of the original Constitution. Yet the claim would be far less significant without the second text. Despite *Marbury v. Madison,* the Court is likely to have remained, without the second text, the weakest, "the least dangerous," of the three branches of government.[2] Ironically, the Court has been strengthened not only with regard to the president and the Congress but also with regard to civil society itself. What the state machine protects it can also subvert. The greater the power to protect, the greater the power to subvert.

It is hard now to imagine what the first text would be like without the second, the Constitution without the Bill of Rights (or with the Bill only as a hortatory addendum). The political machine would certainly be different, and so might the society be that it organizes and protects. But perhaps that society, even as it was at the end of the eighteenth century, required the Bill; required just this inscription of rights; wrote, so to speak, its own ticket. We have a Bill of Rights because we have a diverse and pluralistic society. It's not that the Bill is

2 Alexander Hamilton, *Federalist* 78.

functional to the society but rather that it expresses the sensitivities and aspirations of the members. Whether it is actually helpful to them, either as individuals or as a "people," is precisely what is at issue in many constitutional debates. The sensitivities and aspirations are not at issue. American civil society has its origin in acts of resistance to and flight from religious persecution. The primary purpose of the Bill of Rights is to make such persecution and all its well-remembered political and judicial concomitants impossible. Rights are entitlements to nonconformity and dissidence. The first ten amendments are acts of self-defense on the part of potential nonconformists and dissidents, collective efforts to guarantee diversity; and one may assume that a society capable of such efforts early on would have been capable of them later, too. Still, the textual guarantees are impressive and valuable.

So the Supreme Court became the guardian not of platonic virtue but, in the first instance at least, of Protestant conscience. And given what it means to be conscientious, the justices did not have to convince themselves that particular consciences were virtuous or necessarily right in their protestations in order to conclude that they were worth guarding. Conscience had only to be sincere. Understood in this way, the right of conscience was simply another name for the freedom of the individual. The aura of conscience extended to the whole person, to the mind and spirit that conscience guides, the physical body in which it lives, the home where it is nourished, the activities it inspires. All these are protected as the concentric circles around a sacred center – the individual who shares knowledge (co-science) with God. As the ancient Jews built walls around their Torah, protecting one law with another, so the Americans built walls around the individual, protecting one right with another. The Court guards the walls.

It is commonly said that property is the original right, the right that lies at the heart of the liberal enterprise.[3] Original it probably is so far as early modern legal history goes, but I have come to believe, reading the political and religious literature of the seventeenth and eighteenth centuries, that conscience is theoretically central from the beginning. What makes Lockean self-ownership plausible is the moral self-possession of Protestant men and women, who know, better than anyone else, how they ought to live. They also know, better than anyone else, how they should invest their labor and how they should use the products of their labor. Perhaps these two sorts of knowledge are ideologically as well as theoretically related. I have no reason to deny that the long list of rights reflects economic as well as religious interests. The aura, however, as one might expect, comes from religion, and that is not unimportant. If it serves to strengthen the moral and political claims of property, it also makes it impossible to focus exclusively on those claims. Property belongs to some, conscience to all; property is oligarchic, conscience democratic (or anarchic); given our history, however, the one will always call the other to mind.

The "unencumbered self" of liberal doctrine, so evocatively described by Michael Sandel, bears in its original form the encumbrances of divinity; and it derives from those encumbrances the larger part of its attraction.[4] The individual is bound to his God – the singular possessive pronoun is very important – and unencumbered only with reference to his fellow men. "Whatsoever hopes or obligations I should be bound with," an English radical of the 1640s told Oliver

3 The standard example of this argument is C. B. Macpherson, *The Political Theory of Possessive Individualism: Hobbes to Locke* (Oxford: The Clarendon Press, 1962).

4 Michael J. Sandel, *Liberalism and the Limits of Justice* (Cambridge: Cambridge University Press, 1982).

Cromwell, "if afterwards God should reveal himself, I would break it speedily, if it were an hundred a day."[5] It is because of his close and personal relation to God that someone like that is capable of "protestantism" in every other relation. The list of obligations and impositions against which conscientious men and women have protested is very long: church attendance, religious oaths, military conscription, censorship, tithes and taxes, expropriation and eminent domain, public health laws, paternalistic regulation, marriage vows, and so on. Some of these protests are successful, others are not; some of them may be divinely authorized, others, we can safely assume, are not; they are all made possible by the existence of an individual putatively tied to God and then constitutionally authorized to have scruples about every other tie.

This authorization is conservative in its consequences insofar as the Bill of Rights reflects the actually existing civil society and insofar as individuals are already possessed of their rights: holding in their hands whatever it is they take to be rightfully theirs, free in fact from all the bonds that they regard as illegitimate. In theoretical terms, the Constitution turns the privileged position of such individuals into a matter of law; in practical terms, it fortifies positions that might otherwise be radically exposed to the assaults of democratic majorities (although these assaults have turned out to be less dangerous than expected). The case is clearest with regard to property owners, where a rights-oriented interpretation of the due process clause made possession, unless it came by way of force or fraud, into a legal and moral entitlement that was effective for deades against strongly based reform movements. But there are

---

5 A. S. P. Woodhouse, ed., *Puritanism and Liberty* (London: J. M. Dent and Sons, 1938), pt. 1 ("The Putney Debates"), p. 34.

other examples. Consider the extraordinary longevity of the original assignment of conscientious objector status (by most of the thirteen states) to the enrolled members of certain explicitly named Protestant sects. Today's members possess those rights as a virtual inheritance, and because of this possession it has been difficult to claim the same or similar rights for anyone else. If for much of its history the Supreme Court was the defender of the economic status quo, it was also, though more intermittently, the defender of the religious status quo. And the same defense extended to the social status quo, represented by the combined rights of worship, assembly, petition, due process, trial by one's peers, and so on. So constitutional conservatism sustains something like the civil society of the eighteenth century even in the face of industrial revolution, mass immigration, urbanization, cold war – changes not only in the scope but also in the very character of our common life.

Social Change

Conservatism must be the crucial feature of any written constitution. Why write it down except to give the machinery it designs and the principles it proclaims stability over the long haul? And yet the Constitution is also a radical document, opening the way for, if not actually stimulating, social change. I want to turn now to the subversive logic of rights, which is, I suppose, the currently fashionable topic, though it is not fashion alone that dictates the turn. In the last several decades, in politics and jurisprudence alike, the Constitution's second text has come fully into its own. Instead of a set of restraints on the operation of the state machine, the Bill

111

of Rights is more and more taken to describe the purpose of the machine. Once it was said that the government must not violate individual rights as it goes about its business. Now it is said that the chief business of government is to realize individual rights. Rights these days are less things that people actually have than things that they have a right to have – and therefore ought to have *right now.*[6] What lies behind this sea-change is the discovery (and the self-discovery) of the invisible men and women of twentieth-century civil society. For these people, the first text of the Constitution provides an agency, and the second text a mandate, for social change.

So the Constitution facilitates the defense but also the transformation of civil society. I want to look now at four different sorts of social and political action through which the transformation is attempted. Though the list is logically neat, I don't claim that it is exhaustive. It begins with civil society, then moves on to the state, on the assumption that the transformative work is commonly initiated by individuals and groups who then seek the help of one or another part of the governmental machine.

First, collective action to alter the existing patterns of ownership, hierarchy, command and obedience: the work of parties and mass movements. Here the Bill of Rights functions primarily to enable groups of citizens to assemble, organize, petition, and so on. But it is also said, as in the civil rights movement, for example, that oppressed and excluded men and women don't in fact enjoy the rights enumerated in the Bill and will never enjoy them until the social order has been transformed. So the Bill provides a reason as well as an enabling framework for transformation. The most significant fact about

6 See the arguments of Ronald Dworkin, *Taking Rights Seriously* (Cambridge, Mass.: Harvard University Press, 1977).

political action of this sort, however, is its relative lack of success. Despite many beginnings, moments of high hope, and
real achievements along the way, the social order and all its
hierarchies are more or less intact. One reason for this (relative)
failure is the very diversity of civil society and the protection
accorded to diversity by the Bill of Rights. This group, let's say,
supports a certain reform; another group opposes it; and both
act with equal right (to assemble, organize, petition, and so on)
even if one side is "right" in terms of rights theory. Another
perhaps more important reason is that diversity does not
express itself only in differences of opinion but also in differences in power. Enabling is equal, but in most cases of political
or social conflict the two sides are not equally able. Effective
political organization requires resources as well as constitutional entitlements – and those who already have resources are
likely to be constitutionally entitled to them. So the conservatism of rights subverts their inherent subversiveness.

Second, individual action to alter one's own relationships
without waiting for a more general social transformation. If
collective action takes the form that Albert Hirschman calls
"voice," individual action commonly takes the form of
"exit."[7] It is marked by a radically individualist and separatist
spirit: emigration, secession, divorce, resignation, disengagement. The spirit, again, has religious origins – in the idea of a
conscience that can never be locked up, tied down, coerced or
bound, except with reference to a personal God. The post-
Protestant individual claims a similar freedom, usually without the exception. Privacy is the most cherished individual
right, and it is on its behalf that the Supreme Court has shaped
a new right "constructively" out of all the explicit rights of the

7 Albert Hirschman, *Exit, Voice, and Loyalty: Responses to Decline in Firms, Organizations, and States* (Cambridge, Mass.: Harvard University Press, 1970).

Bill and guaranteed the integrity of a private realm. The construction seems legitimate enough; one can't protect rights of association without acknowledging rights of dissociation. But just as the "unencumbered self" of liberal theory was once thought to bear the encumbrances of God, so it has ever since been thought ready and willing to encumber itself. If men and women protested against one obligation, they assumed another; left one church, joined another; divorced one spouse, married another. It would be a very great change indeed in the pattern of social relationships if the "unencumbered self" of theory were to emerge in practice as the radically unattached individual—standing alone but with the very best legal standing, the ward, as it were, of the Court.

Third, governmental action for the sake of social reform or transformation (seconding and supporting the collective efforts of parties and movements within civil society). This is exactly the sort of action that was supposed to be constrained by the Bill of Rights, the second text setting limits on the powers created by the first, without however making it impossible to exercise those powers. But the government can act on behalf of rights as well as subject to their constraint. The classic example in recent times is the enforcement of school desegregation in the name of "equal protection." Wherever rights are systematically violated, government officials must seek a systematic remedy, and it is unlikely that the remedy can consist entirely of prohibitions and preventions. Positive action will commonly be required, institutional rearrangements, new regulatory policies and social practices. Given the regime of checks and balances, this sort of thing is achieved, if it is achieved at all, very slowly. Competing interests inside the state machine, like competing interests in civil society, inhibit social transformation.

Fourth, governmental action for the sake of individual freedom (seconding and supporting private efforts). What is
involved here is precisely prohibition and prevention, the
annulment of repressive legislation, the hindrance of hin-
drances to free choice and private willfulness. Here the Court
has been the most important agency, authorized by the second text to oppose all other agencies of government. Its
achievements are impressive: it has banned prayer in the
public schools, legalized abortion, virtually abolished the
censorship of art and literature, extended the right of conscientious objection to nonreligious persons, established the
private realm. Other agencies are also active, as in recent
legislation (at the state rather than the federal level) reform-
ing the procedures for divorce and divorce settlements, so as
to make divorce much easier than it once was and also, apparently, to shift resources from families and children to single individuals, mostly men.[8] One can be happy or unhappy
about these achievements or happy about some and unhappy about others, but they do derive in a fairly consistent
way from the second text: they are generated by taking
rights and the rights-bearing individual seriously. As soon as
one does that, the rights that we actually exercise fade in significance before the rights that we might exercise, if only
the powerful machine provided by the first text can be har-
nessed for the job.

What this brief survey suggests is the strongly individualist
bias that the second text introduces into the Constitution as a
whole. Of course, it is generally true in every human society
that individuals are more capable of changing their own situa-
tion than of changing the social order, but I don't think that
there are many societies in which the possibilities for individ-

8 See Lenore Weitzman, *The Divorce Revolution* (New York: Free Press, 1986).

ual change are so large and so radical that they function as a
virtual substitute for social change. Nor can there be many
societies in which the government, as incapable in the United
States as anywhere else of structural reform, can so easily be
enlisted in defense of individual freedom, that is to say, in defense of protest, separation, and privacy. Of the four sorts of
action that I have described, the second and fourth, where single individuals are the active agents or immediate beneficia-
ries, are culturally preferred and constitutionally favored –
most likely, therefore, to be effective. It is easy enough to think
of individuals and whole classes of individuals for whom they
are not (yet) effective, whose rights are not (yet) taken seriously. But the social and constitutional tendency is clear.

We might describe that tendency, programmatically, in the
language of "critical legal theory." It represents, as Roberto
Unger writes of his own program, a "super-liberalism" which
"pushes the liberal premises about state and society, about
freedom from dependence and governance of social relations
by the will, to the point at which they merge into a large ambi-
tion: the building of a social world less alien to a self that can
always violate the generative rules of its own mental or social
constructs."[9] This is the old Protestant scheme restated (in
state-of-the-art theoretical language), with the same isolated
individual at the center, who can always scruple at doing
what, only a short time ago, he solemnly promised to do. It
seems that the individual is known now by his will rather than
his conscience, but he poses familiar problems nonetheless.
Doesn't the dissidence of his dissent, the constant violation of
generative rules, get in the way of the larger enterprise, "building a social world"? Unger hedges his bets when he hopes for

9 Roberto Unger, *The Critical Legal Studies Movement* (Cambridge, Mass.: Harvard University Press, 1986), p. 41.

nothing more than a world "less alien" to the eternally trans-gressive self. Indeed, it is hard to imagine any sort of *social* world in which this self won't be constrained to some degree, in which, therefore, he won't continue to feel himself alien, something less than Rousseau's citizen bound only by his own will. What is the program, then, for this "something less"? What account can we give of the legitimate constraints on dis-sidence and violation?

Promoting Pluralism

We might respond to these questions simply by pointing to the first text of the Constitution. There the government is authorized to tax its citizens, to punish them for violating its laws, to regulate their commercial relations, to raise armies and make war. But this just describes the capabilities of the machine; it doesn't tell us how it is to be operated or for what ends. The ends described in the preamble are too inclusive to be very helpful: "establish Justice, insure domestic Tranquil-ity, provide for the common Defense, promote the general Welfare, and secure the Blessings of Liberty for ourselves and our posterity." On a certain reading of the liberal tradition, the last two of these stand in sharp contradiction to one another: the more liberty is secured for individuals, the less general will welfare be. I don't want to insist that this is the only correct reading of the tradition, but certainly the actual experience of protestantism, separatism, and privatization makes it hard to say what an adjective like "general," or even a plural pronoun like "our," might mean. Is there anything that is so importantly general, so deeply ours, that we might for its sake discourage protest, separation, and privacy?

A hard question. I assume that most Americans are not pre-pared – certainly, I am not – to give up any of the rights enumerated in the second text. But one of the chief reasons for valuing those rights, it seems to me, is that they facilitate the first and third forms, the collective and cooperative forms, of social action. They enable groups of citizens who share some religious or political or economic understanding or interest to organize themselves, to act on their understanding and defend their interest. They open the way for ideological disagreement and collective self-assertion. They make possi-ble what is currently called "the politics of difference." For the assumption of the Constitution, of the two texts taken together, is that, Americans will have different ideas, first of all about eternal life and salvation and then about the preamble's list: justice, tranquility, defense, welfare, and liberty. The the-oretical justification for these differences is individualist in character; hence the bias of the text. But the expected activity was collective: when one asserts "the right of the people peacefully to assemble," one expects assemblies – not litigious individuals tracked by lawyers, but gatherings, meetings, cau-cuses, and party conventions; not legal argument, but politi-cal debate; not briefs, but pamphlets.

The privatizing effects of the Bill of Rights were almost cer-tainly not anticipated by the authors of the Bill. What they had in mind, as I have already suggested, was the existing diversity of American society. This was indeed a separatist society, composed, that is, of people who had literally sepa-rated themselves from Old World states and churches. Once again, these people justified their separation on grounds of private conscience, the moral knowledge each one of them shared with his God. In practice, however, they shared this knowledge among themselves too. And so the diversity to which they gave rise was a diversity of groups. The groups rested on individual consent, but they *rested* on consent with some confidence and security. That's why it was so easy to assign conscientious objector status on the basis of membership.[10] The separatism of American life did not mean, or was not taken to mean, that Americans were frivolous in their associations. On the contrary, they made weighty decisions and formed stable groups; hence the actions of these groups, their assemblies and petitions and, by extension, their rallies, demonstrations, marches, and strikes, were worthy of constitutional protection. Individuals with consciences and interests formed groups with purposes. And since the purpose of many of these groups was and is to convince the rest of us to live in a certain way, to think of justice, tranquility, and so on, in these terms rather than those, the socializing effects of conscience and interest are extensive and far-reaching.

Yet this is true only so long as it seems both necessary and possible to convince the rest of us to live in a certain way. There is always this alternative: to live that way oneself "without tarrying for the magistrate," as seventeenth-century Protestants argued – or for anyone else. Despite its anticipation of collective action, the Constitution has turned out to favor something else, nicely summed up in the twentieth-century maxim about "doing your own thing." Imagine now a civil society founded on this maxim, a literal diversity of individuals, this one and that one and that one and that one, not an assembly or a congregation or a community but something more like what Sartre calls a "series."[11] Of course, doing your own thing does not mean living in isolation, for some of the things one

10 Michael Walzer, *Obligations: Essays on Disobedience, War, and Citizenship* (Cambridge, Mass.: Harvard University Press, 1970), chap. 6.

11 Jean-Paul Sartre, *Critique of Dialectical Reason, I, Theory of Practical Ensembles*, trans. Allan Sheridan-Smith (London: N.L.B., 1976), pp. 256ff.

wants to do can't be done alone. People will still come together for conversation, love, worship, and even the defense of common interests. But these unions are likely to be temporary and unstable, given the radical individualism on which they are based. The example of religious cultism in the United States today suggests that they are also likely to be frivolous. Cults are as entitled to constitutional protection as churches and congregations; we would not want a governmental office set up to distinguish between serious and silly religiosity. But that is not a reason to rejoice in the advance of silliness. Similarly, the growing number of people living alone – living in "single person households," in the census phrase – are entitled to exactly the same protection that families get against, say, "unreasonable searches and seizures," but that is no reason to rejoice in the advance of solitude and dissociation.

A Sartrean "series," a dissociated society, is a limiting case. Sartre's example is a queue, and the example makes it obvious that a whole society organized on the serial principle is not possible: without some background solidarity, every queue would turn into a melee. Similarly, a society composed entirely of single-person households and religious cults would have no cohesion at all, would not, in fact, be a "society." I am describing tendencies, not established realities. Still, it is worth asking what resistance we can put up to these tendencies.

It is not the divisiveness of dissociation that is worrying. Rousseau argued long ago that if a society had to be divided, then multiplying the divisions would reduce their force and salience: a host of secondary associations is second best to none at all.[12] In my limiting case, however, the host equals the total number of citizens; every individual member of society

12 Jean-Jacques Rousseau, *The Social Contract,* trans G. D. H. Cole (New York: E. P. Dutton, 1950), bk. 2, chap. 3.

is self-associated, primary in his own eyes, secondary in everyone else's. The conflicts among individuals are then too dispersed and trivial to threaten the stability of social life, but they are also too dispersed and trivial to energize social life. A society in which political parties, interest groups, and religious communities quarrel about the common defense and the general welfare is, however bitter the quarrels, a society whose members are forced to think about what is common and what is general. They are mobilized for democratic politics, that is, for public work of many different kinds, more or less useful, more or less interesting to their fellows; whereas in a dissociated society all work is apolitical, private, and (mostly) uninteresting.

Is there some way to bring rights-bearing individuals together, to enhance the possibilities for collective action? Here the Supreme Court is not likely to be much help; the second text that it enforces doesn't press in this direction, whatever the anticipation of its authors. Consulting a lawyer and writing a brief will not right now (though it sometimes might) advance the cause of association. Perhaps the Constitution as a whole, conceived as the sacred text of a civil religion, might help. Indeed, the Constitution is the sacred text of our civil religion, but the seminary in which the text is studied, expounded, and interpreted is the law school; the chief ritual observance is litigation; and litigation serves most importantly to enhance the second and fourth forms, the privatizing forms, of social action. We can, of course, celebrate the diversity that the Constitution fosters and protects. It is harder to celebrate radical dissociation. Can we be knit together by our mutual acceptance of difference? A society that respects individualism and pluralism can also respect itself and value the legal structure through which it operates. I am less sure about a society whose members are merely tolerant of (or resigned to) each other's isolation. Are they grateful to be allowed, when they please, to part company and be left alone, or do they yearn (secretly) for an unconstitutional solidarity?

Yearnings like that can be dangerous, and yet I want to argue that a decent society requires not only individual rights but also group solidarities and the pluralist and democratic politics that groups make possible. Democracy itself is a value sufficiently general and sufficiently ours to warrant state action against the long-term effects of privatization. If the Court defends and extends the regime of rights, then perhaps it is the task of Congress to look for ways of strengthening the internal life, the jurisdictional reach, and the cohesiveness of secondary associations. I have no list of measures in mind; I would only recall the way in which the Wagner Act facilitated the organization of labor unions in the 1930s or the way in which matching grants to private welfare agencies have made it possible today for religious groups to run an extensive system of daycare centers, hospitals, and nursing homes. The Constitution is biased toward individual rights, and perhaps it should be; but constitutional power exists to balance the bias or to counter some of its effects. And just as the Court's commitment to rights generates new rights and pushes separatism beyond the actually existing separateness of civil society, so Congress's commitment to group solidarity ought to generate new groupings and new experiences of collective action: worker-owned factories, health cooperatives, experimental schools, neighborhood alliances, and so on.

It should not be the goal of congressional action, however, to create a single, all-encompassing solidarity. That was what the Bill of Rights, and especially the First Amendment with its no-establishment clause, was designed to prevent – for the sake of a civil society that is probably still lively and diverse enough to resist the creation. The Bill was designed, indeed, to protect the existing states as well as the existing churches, interest groups, and families, and perhaps we need to look again to our federalist past if we are to revitalize associational life. The states do not seem at this moment the best possible units for collective action, but no one can predict at what level of politics or society the best units might be found. We have to ask: where is there some effective demand for organizational structure and common effort? Where might there be an enthusiastic response to governmental initiative? Where are the creative forces in our society that might benefit, as the labor movement once benefited, from political authorization? Insofar as these questions have answers, we have a political agenda and a constitutional structure within which to pursue it. If it ever happens that they have no answers, we are probably beyond constitutional help.

I argued at the beginning of this essay that the original Constitution designed a state and the Bill of Rights reflected a society. The purpose of the Bill was to make the constituent elements of that society inaccessible to the state. Its authors thought those elements, rights-bearing individuals, above all, to be strong and creative. Today those same individuals, carrying those same rights (or new rights of the same sort), look very different: dissociation renders them weak and passive. So it makes sense to call the state to the rescue of civil society and then to search for effective means of rescue – for the state is the only constitutionally specified agent of collective action and the only agent that might, conceivably, be pregnant with additional agents. I need only say, finally, that when the state acts in this way it can only act subject to its internal checks and balances, which now include all the rights that the Court enforces. But I don't think it is merely a political trick (though it may be tricky) to look for ways of limiting protestantism, separatism, and privatization without violating individual rights.

ACKNOWLEDGEMENTS

These essays were first brought together (without "Constitutional Rights") by Nadia Urbinati in a little book published by Marsilio in Italy (1991), which she edited, translated, and introduced. Her introduction was aimed at Italian readers, and it does not appear here, but this book exists only because of her.

My own introduction to the Italian book has been extensively re-written for the American edition. The other essays have all appeared elsewhere; I have done some minor editing for the sake of consistency, but have made no effort to eliminate the repetition of central themes. "Civility and Civic Virtue" and "What Does It Mean" were published in the journal *Social Research* (1974 and 1990). "What Does It Mean" was first presented as the Morgan Lecture at Dickinson College, Carlisle, Pennsylvania in 1989. "Constitutional Rights" was written for a conference held at DePauw University, Greencastle, Indiana in 1987 (and read also, in that bicentennial year, at meetings in Jerusalem and Bologna). It was subsequently published, along with other conference papers, by the University Press of Kansas in a volume edited by Robert E. Calvert, who also organized the DePauw conference. My "Pluralism" essay appeared in that remarkable book *The Harvard Encyclopedia of American Ethnic Groups,* and would never have been written but for the prompting and encouragement of one of its editors, Stephan Thernstrom. I am grateful to all the publishers and editors who have kept me writing, who saw to the publication of these essays, and who consented to their re-publication.

WHAT IT MEANS TO BE AN AMERICAN
was printed and bound by Data Reproduction Corp.
of Rochester Hills, Michigan. Jackets were printed by
New England Book Components of Hingham, Massachusetts.
The text is set in Adobe Stone Serif, with Adobe Stone Sans Serif for
display, with 10 $1/4$ point type on 15 point leading.
Designed and typeset by Deborah Zeidenberg
on Quark XPress for the Macintosh.